ISLAM IN THE WEST

"Even if they put the sun in my right hand and the moon in my left hand, I would not take off my veil."

"Australians, yes, Muslims too."

OMAR HASSAN

First Published in Australia in 2026
O. Hassan
All correspondences:
Omar.hassan60@hotmail.com

National Library of Australia
Pre-Publication Data Service (PDS)
NLApp118918

Islam in the West.

ISBN 978 – 0 – 646 – 73514 – 6.

1. Islam - 21st century - Social aspects.

To You alone, O my Creator
If someday, somewhere, someone is guided because of this humble effort, then You have granted me Your mercy and made my life worthwhile on this earth.
All I ask of You is to grant me and my progeny a place in Paradise

Preface

This book emerges from lived experience, long observation, and deep reflection on migration, identity, and belonging. It does not seek to provide a definitive account of Australia or of migration itself, but rather to explore the emotional and social realities encountered by many who arrive in a new country with hope and expectation.

Migration is not merely a physical journey; it is an ongoing negotiation between past and present, identity and acceptance, memory and survival. The reflections in this work aim to give voice to experiences that are often discussed privately but rarely examined openly.

This book is written for readers willing to engage with complexity—to sit with discomfort, contradiction, and unanswered questions. Its purpose is not to accuse or condemn, but to invite thought, conversation, and deeper understanding of how societies receive those who arrive seeking dignity and belonging.

Islam in the West presents a faith-based critique of contemporary Western political and cultural systems through an Islamic moral lens. The book argues that modern global power structures prioritise control, materialism, and surveillance while eroding spiritual accountability and justice.

Drawing on religious belief, historical interpretation, and social observation, the author challenges secular governance, media influence, economic dominance, and cultural narratives, contrasting them with Islamic concepts of morality, purpose, and accountability. The work positions Islam not as a political movement, but as a comprehensive ethical framework addressing the moral vacuum the author perceives in modern civilisation.

Foreword

This book is not written to comfort. It is written to confront.

We live in an age where power no longer announces itself openly. It operates quietly, through systems rather than armies, through influence rather than force, and through compliance rather than consent. Decisions that shape the lives of billions are increasingly made far from those who must live with their consequences. The language of freedom remains, but its substance is steadily eroded.

Globalisation is often described as inevitable, neutral, and beneficial. Yet inevitability should never exempt an idea from scrutiny. History teaches that systems presented as progress can, when left unchallenged, become instruments of injustice. This book examines globalisation not as a technical process, but as a moral and civilisational question.

The arguments presented here are not claims of secret knowledge, nor accusations disguised as facts. They are a critique—grounded in observation, belief, and moral reasoning—of a world order that increasingly prioritises control over conscience, uniformity over diversity, and power over accountability.

At its core, this work asks a simple but urgent question: **Who decides the direction of humanity?** Governments? Institutions? Markets? Or principles that stand above all of them?

From an Islamic perspective, the answer is clear. Justice does not originate in power, but in truth. Authority does not belong to those who possess force, wealth, or influence, but to those who are bound by moral responsibility. Islam is presented here not as a cultural identity, but as a comprehensive ethical framework—one that challenges any system that places human ambition above divine guidance.

Whether the reader agrees or disagrees, this book demands engagement rather than dismissal. It invites reflection in a time when reflection is discouraged, and conviction in an era that rewards silence.

The future will not be shaped by systems alone. It will be shaped by what people are willing to question—and what they are willing to defend.

Author's Note

This book is a work of belief, analysis, and conviction. It does not claim to speak for all Muslims, nor does it seek to impose agreement. It presents a perspective—rooted in faith, informed by observation, and driven by concern for the direction in which the world is moving.

All political, social, and economic commentary in this book is expressed as critique and opinion. It addresses systems and ideas, not individuals. Where historical or contemporary events are referenced, they are discussed for the purpose of moral and philosophical examination, not accusation.

The reader is encouraged to approach this work thoughtfully. Agreement is not required, but honesty is. The issues raised—power, control, justice, family, faith, and responsibility—affect all people, regardless of culture or belief.

Islam, as presented here, is not portrayed as a tool of domination, but as a system of accountability. It demands restraint from the powerful, protection for the weak, and responsibility from the individual. In a world increasingly governed by interests rather than principles, this message is both uncomfortable and necessary.

This book was written because silence has become too easy, and questioning has become too rare. If it unsettles, it has achieved its purpose. If it provokes reflection, it has gone further still.

The future belongs not to those who control the world, but to those who understand what it is for.

Why This Book Had to Be Written

This book had to be written because silence allows misunderstanding to harden into normality.

Migration is often discussed in numbers, policies, and slogans, yet the inner cost of displacement—the quiet erosion of identity, dignity, and belonging—is rarely addressed with honesty. Many of these experiences are endured privately, spoken of only within families or not at all. Over time, what is left unsaid becomes invisible.

This work exists to name what is frequently felt but seldom articulated: the pressure to erase oneself in order to belong, the subtle ways exclusion operates, and the long-term emotional consequences of being treated as permanently provisional. These realities are not always dramatic, but they are cumulative. They shape lives, families, and generations.

The book was also written to challenge simplified narratives. Nations are neither purely welcoming nor purely hostile; they are complex, contradictory, and evolving. To examine those contradictions is not an act of disloyalty, but of engagement. Honest critique is a form of participation, not rejection.

For those who have lived these experiences, this book offers recognition rather than instruction. For those who have not, it offers an opportunity to listen without defensiveness. Understanding does not require agreement, but it does require attention.

This book had to be written because belonging should not require erasure. A society grows stronger when it can hold multiple histories, identities, and truths without demanding silence from those who arrive in hope.

Finally, this is a book that can, indeed, be judged by its cover.

Legal Disclaimer:

This book is a work of non-fiction reflection and social commentary. All views expressed are the author's own and are presented as opinion, interpretation, and personal experience.
It represents the author's religious beliefs, interpretations, and moral critiques of historical events, media behaviour, power structures, political and social systems. It does not advocate harm, violence, or hostility toward individuals or groups. Any references to institutions, governments, or ideologies are expressions of opinion and belief.
Descriptions of events, attitudes, or experiences are based on personal perception and are not presented as comprehensive or universal representations.
This book is intended for informational and reflective purposes only and should not be construed as legal, political, or professional advice.

The Author
Omar Hassan

CONTENTS

(1)

LEAVING HOME
What Is the Price?

When many people decide to leave their homeland and move to a country like Australia to make it their home, they often fail to understand the conditions associated with the permission granted to them to live there. They live under the illusion that they are getting something for nothing. They imagine that they have been welcomed because of their skills, values, or experience, or because they have something meaningful to contribute.

They believe they have been given a chance by a civilised, advanced, and wealthy Western country that cares about them as human beings, and that at last they are about to realise their dreams. They believe they will be treated with dignity, own a home and a car, send their children to private schools, receive hospital care, obtain medicine when they are sick, and finally have someone wipe away their tears, and finally experiencing relief from hardship.

They were wrong.

People are not invited to countries like Australia because they are valued. They are permitted entry under conditions they are never encouraged to understand, attached to residency and long-term settlement. Many arrive with high expectations, believing that opportunity alone guarantees stability, security, and dignity.

For some, these expectations are not realised.

Permission to live here is not generosity. It is control.

And most people only realise that after it is too late.

The conditions attached to residency are not designed to help newcomers succeed; they are designed to keep them compliant. The promise of opportunity is used as leverage. Gratitude is demanded. Silence is expected.

Those who question the system are reminded—subtly at first, then aggressively—that they are replaceable.

Many never imagine that finding stable employment—work that provides dignity, self-respect, and security—could be extremely difficult or even unattainable. Some live for decades without ever securing employment that offers long-term stability or social mobility. The emotional impact of this reality can extend beyond the individual, affecting family relationships and self-worth.

In some households, unemployment or underemployment becomes a hidden burden. Parents may conceal their struggles from their children or spouses, hoping to protect them from worry or disappointment.

Many never anticipate the instability of housing, or the stress of living week to week. The loss of accommodation due to unpaid rent, the inability to maintain an ageing vehicle, or the constant fear of unexpected expenses becomes a lived reality for some families.

Healthcare access, while available, may not always meet expectations. Families may experience frustration when medical concerns are not immediately resolved or when treatment costs place additional strain on limited finances. These moments can be especially distressing when children are involved.

Poverty often reveals itself quietly: worn clothing, delayed necessities, difficult choices between essentials. Some parents stretch limited resources in ways they never imagined, simply to get through each day.

Food insecurity, isolation from extended family, and the inability to afford travel home deepen the sense of separation. For earlier generations, even communication with loved ones overseas was limited by cost, leading to emotional distance and loneliness.

Parents may worry about their children's future—education, employment prospects, and vulnerability to negative influences. The fear that children may struggle or drift away from family values weighs heavily on many.

They never imagine their children having no real chance in education or employment, ending up on the streets, using drugs, and dying before them.

The loss of a child—whether through estrangement, circumstance, or tragedy—is an experience that time does not erase. Explanations and procedures may exist, but emotional resolution often does not.

Many came seeking a better future for their children. Their children were their greatest hope and motivation. When that hope feels compromised, the cost of migration can seem immeasurable.

For some, the price is not only financial, but emotional, relational, and generational. It is a cost paid quietly, over a lifetime, in ways that are rarely acknowledged or fully understood.

Where did it all go—the nice house, the beautiful car, the private schools?

They did not understand that the deal was not free and that there was a price to pay for being accepted into this country.

The promised symbols of success—comfort, stability, upward mobility—may feel increasingly distant.

Then what happens?

Over time, some come to realise that migration involved costs they did not fully foresee. The emotional and social price can be significant, particularly when family life is shaped by long working hours, shift work, and exhaustion. When parents are rarely present, children may spend more time under institutional or social influence than family guidance.

Income, when earned, is often absorbed by the high cost of living: housing, utilities, transport, insurance, education expenses, and basic necessities. Financial pressure becomes a constant presence. Missing payments can have serious consequences, adding further stress.

Life can begin to feel structured around survival rather than growth. Many feel they work simply to maintain existence, with little opportunity to build savings or security.

Despite these struggles, migrants are often reminded that they live in a fortunate country and should feel grateful. Comparisons to others who face greater danger or hardship can leave individuals feeling unheard or dismissed when they express difficulty.

Returning home is not always an option. Financial constraints, lost assets, or the absence of a place to return to can make departure impossible. For some, acknowledging the gap between expectations and reality is deeply painful.

Long-term physical and emotional strain may take a toll, particularly for those who worked in demanding or hazardous environments. The consequences of such labour may emerge years later.

Even after death, financial obligations can remain, placing further burden on families.

Some parents eventually decide to leave, hoping to reclaim family unity. Others remain, watching their children grow increasingly distant as external influences replace parental presence.

Modern systems of welfare, education, and housing may offer support, but they can also unintentionally weaken family bonds by reducing dependence on parental authority. This shift can leave parents feeling powerless and grieving a loss that is difficult to articulate.

Many parents reflect with regret, questioning the choices they made and the environment in which they raised their children. Grief, guilt, and self-blame can become overwhelming.

Everything is designed to ensure no money is left. Money is power, and not everyone is allowed to have that power. You are charged for everything—even for things you do not want, need, or use. The only thing you are not charged for is the air you breathe, but even that may change.

Despite all this suffering, you are constantly told you live in "the lucky country" and should feel grateful to be there. You are reminded of others who risk their lives to come just to work, pay bills, and survive. You are made to doubt yourself, and if you complain, you are told, *"If you don't like it, go back to where you came from."*

Why don't people go back?

Many cannot afford the ticket to leave. Many cling to the illusion that one more week of hard work will change things. Many have nowhere to go. They sold everything to come here; coming here cost them their lifetime savings. Being here is the only asset they own. Who will buy it back? Who will compensate them for what they lost?

Many would rather deny the mistake than face the truth—a truth that can be fatal to those who worked in dangerous conditions, exposed to chemicals and asbestos.

Bills continue even after death. If no one can pay for burial, bodies are kept until someone finds the money.

They did not realise the true price was their children. Many could not endure it. Some left suddenly, desperate to save their children at any cost. Others watched helplessly as their children slipped away day by day.

It is a system designed to break families, destroy unity, and eliminate any power a united family might represent.

The system makes it easy for children to leave their parents—providing shelter, allowances, drugs, and isolation from parental authority. Parents watch their children die, forgiving each other through tears.

Many parents cannot forgive themselves for coming here or for raising children here. After losing their children, many lose their own lives to grief.

No parent can forgive or forget receiving the body of their child, knowing parts were taken from that body.

Under a corrupt legal system, there is always an explanation, always a way out for those responsible. Time is expected to erase everything—but it never does.

They came here for their children. Their children were their only asset, their greatest treasure. And this is the price demanded in return for living here.

It is a lifetime of destruction, a tragedy beyond measure—a crime of the century. A system without mercy, heart, or comprehension. A system of wolves.

Education: Where Futures Are Decided for You

The education system no longer rewards ability. It enforces obedience.

Final external examinations once limited interference. They allowed talent to speak for itself. That protection has been deliberately dismantled. Outcomes are now controlled through year-long assessments administered by teachers who answer to government directives.

This is not reform. It is centralised control.

A student's future can now be destroyed quietly, incrementally, and without accountability. One biased assessment is enough. One teacher's opinion is enough. There is no appeal that matters, no reset that works, no second chance that changes the outcome. Repeating a year does not correct injustice—it entrenches it.

This system decides who will become doctors, lawyers, engineers, and academics—and who will never be allowed near those professions. It filters populations. It excludes entire groups without ever admitting it is doing so.

Parents have been deliberately sidelined. Their authority is treated as an inconvenience. Their concerns are dismissed. Their children are conditioned to see the state—not family—as the ultimate authority.

By the time parents realise what has happened, the damage is irreversible.

Justice: Where Victims Are Punished and Criminals Are Protected

The justice system does not fail by accident. It fails by design.

Criminals are released repeatedly, emboldened by a system that shields them from consequences. Victims, meanwhile, are priced out of justice before they even reach a courtroom. Lawyers demand money first. Truth comes later—if at all.

Most victims never see accountability. They see paperwork, delays, dismissals, and indifference.

Defend yourself in your own home and you risk becoming the criminal. Allow yourself to be robbed and you are told that is the price of living in a "civil society."

Children watch their parents submit. They learn early that the law does not protect the innocent—it disciplines the compliant.

This is not justice. It is managed victimhood.

Elections: Compulsion Masquerading as Democracy

If voting were optional, the system would collapse overnight.

Compulsory voting exists to hide contempt. People are forced to attend elections they do not believe in, to choose between candidates they do not trust, to legitimise outcomes they had no real role in shaping. Rejection votes are meaningless. Ballots disappear into opaque processes. Counting systems are inaccessible, unverifiable, and conveniently complex. Outcomes are negotiated, not chosen. Power rotates between approved players. Policy remains unchanged.

Elections do not decide direction. They assign responsibility.

Media and Foreign Influence: Who Actually Gives the Orders

Governments do not govern independently. They comply.

Foreign interests, financial institutions, and international bodies dictate policy while elected officials perform the role of translators—softening language, inventing justifications, and selling harm as necessity.

The media does not investigate this. It enforces it.

Narratives are synchronised. Dissent is mocked or erased. Journalists who step out of line do not last long. Careers are the reward for obedience.

Leadership changes are staged events. Failures are rebranded as renewals. The public is told change has occurred while policy continues uninterrupted.

This is coordination, not coincidence.

Division, Fear, and the Endgame

A united population is dangerous. A divided one is controllable.

People are split into categories and taught to resent one another. Identity replaces solidarity. Fear replaces trust. Silence replaces speech.

Those who speak plainly are labelled and dismissed. Debate is avoided. Compliance is praised as responsibility.

Eventually, people police themselves. They censor their thoughts, edit their words, and retreat into isolation.

What remains is a population that functions but does not live—educated enough to work, fearful enough to obey, divided enough to never resist.

This is not a broken system.

It is a successful one.

And it will continue exactly as it is until people stop pretending they are free and start acknowledging what has been done to them.

(2)

ARRIVING IN AUSTRALIA
Speak English, or You Will Die

Language, Belonging, and Identity

To those who love Australia, to those who criticise it, and to those who question it

Arrival and First Impressions

(The shock of entry and the beginning of exclusion)

Arriving in Australia for the first time can be a confronting experience. As you enter the airport and approach immigration, you are directed toward two queues: one marked **"Australians"** and the other **"Others."** For someone who has been granted permission to settle here, this moment can raise an immediate and uncomfortable question: *Where do I belong?*

you would automatically ask yourself which queue you should join, and quickly have to make a decision about what you are. *Am I Australian, or am I "Others"?*

The airport, the queues, and the first question: *Where do I belong?*

Initial impressions of power, categorisation, and silent hierarchy.

Australians and Others

How labels are created, enforced, and internalised. Citizenship versus acceptance. it is often noticeable that the queue for Australians moves quickly, while the queue for others progresses more slowly. People in that line may be questioned more extensively or asked to step aside for further checks. Whether intended or not, this experience can leave newcomers with a strong impression that unequal treatment exists from the very first point of entry. From that moment on, before you even enter the country for the first time, you are told and informed that discrimination exists in this country.

New arrivals quickly learn that they are not welcome, especially if they do not speak English well. They are treated rudely and blamed for not learning fast enough, when in reality the problem is ignorance and entitlement.

Discrimination laws exist only on paper, designed to be almost impossible to enforce. Parents endure humiliation for themselves, but discrimination against their children causes lifelong damage.

Discrimination extends beyond certain communities and includes Europeans and New Zealanders, especially during economic downturns.

Language as a Border —English as a gatekeeper to dignity, employment, and respect. Accent, fluency, and the politics of speech.

Becoming Acceptable - The Name You Must Leave Behind

(Pressure to erase the self)

Renaming, mispronunciation, and the loss of identity. Why names matter. Many migrants quickly learn that life becomes easier when they are perceived as "Australian." This perception is not only about citizenship, but also about language, accent, name, and behaviour. Some feel pressure to minimise or hide their background—changing their name, avoiding their native language in public, or distancing themselves from visible cultural practices—in order to be accepted and avoid scrutiny.

If you want things to go smoothly for you, then you must be "Australian." What that means is that you have to forget who you are, where you come from, what your beliefs are, and what language you spoke before. As soon as you can, you must give yourself an Australian name and forget your old one. Your old name was probably too long or too difficult to pronounce, and as soon as that name was called, everyone would look at you twice.

With such a name, you will always be a stranger, a foreigner, and someone who does not belong here.

The Fear of Standing Out

Why difference becomes a liability rather than a strength. For those who do not fit easily into this image, the sense of being an outsider can persist. Accents, unfamiliar names, and different styles of dress can mark a person as foreign long after they have settled, worked, and contributed to society.

People who come to Australia from different countries and cultures may face different kinds of problems while trying to settle here, but at the end of the day, they all share one common experience: they suffer.

Performing Australianness

Dress, behaviour, humour, and imitation as survival strategies. Migrants arrive in Australia from many countries and cultures, each facing unique challenges. Yet many share common struggles: adapting to a new system, securing stable employment, navigating education for their children, and finding a sense of dignity and belonging.
Is Australia truly one nation, united under any ideology? The answer is no. Certain groups call themselves Australians and refer to others by nationality, race, or religion to grant themselves superior rights—even though those others may have arrived earlier. This ignores the real Indigenous people of this land. If Indigenous rights are eliminated, then Afghans who have lived here for over two hundred years would have more claim than anyone else.
Is there a clearly defined Australian identity? Who decides it? On what grounds? Who has the right to take it away?

Words That Wound

(Social language and its consequences)

Some words and labels used in everyday speech, even when dismissed as jokes or slang, can reinforce feelings of exclusion. Such language is often difficult to define precisely, but its intent and effect are widely understood by those on the receiving end. It may be used in response to speaking a language other than English, having a strong accent, or appearing culturally different. Over time, repeated exposure to this kind of language can deeply affect self-worth and confidence.

The Word *wog*, Quite often, it is said when you do or say something that the people using it do not approve of. You may hear it whispered if you attempt to speak a language other than English in public, if you speak with a heavy accent or broken English, or if you dress in a non-Western style. In these circumstances, the word *bloody* usually precedes the word *wog*.

This word is used not only by those who call themselves Aussies, but also by fully imported groups when they see another imported group speaking a different language or dressing differently. They use the word because it makes them feel that they belong here, and because it gains them recognition and approval from the so-called Aussies, signalling that it is acceptable for them to be here.

Many of those imported groups are willing to go far beyond their normal habits of talking, eating, drinking, and dressing to convince themselves that they fit into this society, hoping to prevent the word *wog* from being used against them. In fact, children born here to migrant parents often describe their own parents as wogs when speaking to their peers. Sometimes these children avoid talking to their parents in public out of embarrassment, because their parents come from overseas and do not speak English.

When Migrants Police Migrants

Internalised exclusion and the struggle for approval. In some cases, members of migrant communities themselves adopt these labels and direct them at others. This behaviour can reflect a desire to gain acceptance or demonstrate belonging within the broader society. Unfortunately, it can also deepen divisions and perpetuate the very attitudes that cause harm.

Children of Two Worlds

(The cost paid by the next generation)

Children of migrants may be especially vulnerable. Many grow up balancing two worlds and may feel pressure to distance themselves from their parents' language, clothing, or customs in public spaces. Some experience embarrassment or shame, not because of their families, but because of how difference is treated around them. These experiences can leave lasting emotional effects on both children and parents.

Many children, as a result of the Western system, are encouraged—particularly through the school system—to develop an attitude that makes them ashamed to reveal their real identity, or more precisely, their parents' identity. They refuse to walk next to a mother or father dressed in a way that reveals their place of origin. This tragedy forces many parents to ask themselves, *Where did I go wrong?* It leaves permanent scars on the hearts of migrant parents.

Some children go even further, telling their peers that the parent waiting to pick them up is a neighbour, a babysitter, or a maid. This often occurs when a migrant family attempts to live in an area where they are not considered to belong, or sends their children to a school where they are not considered to belong. In such cases, families are often referred to as *the Greeks*, *the Italians*, or worse, *the Lebanese* or *the Chinese*.

The Migrant Contribution

(What is forgotten or ignored)

Australia has been shaped by migration. People from across the world have contributed labour, knowledge, skills, and culture, helping to build the nation's infrastructure, economy, and institutions. Many arrived fleeing war, poverty, or instability, hoping to provide safety and opportunity for their families.

Yet for some, these hopes are met with disappointment. Secure employment, affordable housing, quality education, and effective social support can be difficult to access. Financial pressure, combined with feelings of exclusion, leads many to question whether the sacrifices they made were worth it.

Many migrants came from civilised countries and brought civilisation to a country that had none of its own. This country was built on the knowledge, education, and experience of migrants.

Those Who Built the Country

Labour, knowledge, skills, and sacrifice.

From War Zones to Worksites

Migration as survival, not opportunity. After living here for some time, many ask: *Where are the good jobs? Where is the education for my children? Where is protection from hunger, homelessness, and starvation?* Where is social security, which turns out to be social insecurity—barely enough to pay bills, leaving nothing to live on? Eventually, many are faced with the question: *Is it all worth it?* For many, going home is no longer an option, so they simply die here.

Fighting a Different War

Economic struggle, housing, and survival in a wealthy nation. Many migrants fled wars, poverty, and starvation, only to arrive here to fight another kind of war—this time their own—while struggling to feed and shelter their families. They fight to protect their children and prevent them from ending up on the streets.

What Is an Australian?

Who defines identity and on what authority?
Australia often presents itself as a unified nation, but debates about identity persist. Questions remain about who defines what it means to be Australian, on what basis, and with what authority. These

discussions frequently overlook the foundational presence and rights of Indigenous peoples, whose connection to the land long predates all others.
Is it worth considering whether the label "Australian," for some, functions as a broad national identity that can obscure deeper histories and cultures—particularly in light of a past shaped by colonisation, land dispossession, the removal of Indigenous children, and policies that sought to marginalise Indigenous peoples?

Labels Without Definitions

How derogatory terms function socially even without formal meaning.
Identity labels—whether based on nationality, culture, or religion—are often applied selectively. For many, maintaining a connection to their heritage is a source of strength and dignity rather than division. Cultural and religious identities have contributed significantly to global civilisation, education, and scientific advancement, and they continue to enrich Australian society today.
If people are allowed to label others by their parents' origins or beliefs, then everyone should be free to label everyone else. From an Arab Muslim perspective, being called Arab and Muslim is an honour. History bears witness to the civilisation Muslims—and Arabs in particular—brought to the world. Europeans once travelled to Muslim Spain for education, while Oxford University still houses books proving that Arabs introduced science and modern mathematics.

Once faith was taken away, conditions reversed. Islam is undermined because of fear of its strength. Calling our children Lebanese or Muslim only reminds us of who we are.

The Lucky Country?

(Reality versus narrative)

Australia is often described as "the lucky country." For some, this description feels accurate. For others, life is marked by hardship, marginalisation, and ongoing struggle. Experiences vary widely depending on background, opportunity, and circumstance.
The taxation system is another injustice: people pay for everything at some of the highest rates in the world, while essential services should be free.
So why do people still pay such high taxes in such a wealthy country, rich in resources, while the majority struggle to survive?

Luck for Whom?

Unequal outcomes in a resource-rich country.
Perhaps it is lucky for some. For many others, it is a nightmare of poverty, discrimination, corruption, drugs, and gambling—protected and promoted by government systems.
New arrivals who struggle with English may encounter impatience or misunderstanding, even though learning a new language takes time and support. While anti-discrimination laws exist, many feel that accessing justice is complex and difficult, particularly when discrimination affects children and families.

Periods of economic stress can intensify social divisions, with resentment directed at migrants or other groups perceived as competitors for jobs or services. At the same time, the cost of living and taxation burden remain ongoing concerns for many residents, especially those who feel they receive limited support in return.

These realities raise important questions: What does fairness truly look like in a diverse society?

How can belonging be built without requiring people to erase who they are?

And how can Australia live up to its ideals for all who call it home?

themes of migration, identity, language, power, and belonging are built around:

Silence in Public Spaces

Why people stop speaking their own languages outside the home.

Ashamed Before They Understand Why

Children absorbing social hierarchies through schools and peers.

Hiding One's Parents

Identity conflict, embarrassment, and emotional distancing.

The Scars That Remain

Long-term psychological effects on families.

ARRIVING IN AUSTRALIA
Speak English, or You Will Die
To those who love Australia, to those who criticise it, and to those who question it,

Questioning the Nation – Questions Australia Must Answer

Final reflections and unresolved challenges.

The Forgotten First Nations

Indigenous presence, erasure, and unresolved injustice.

Identity as Strength, Not Threat

Culture, faith, and historical contribution to civilisation.

Laws That Promise, Systems That Fail

Discrimination protections and practical barriers.

Economic Pressure and Social Blame

How downturns revive old prejudices.

Living Without Permission

Rejecting imposed identities.

Belonging Without Disappearing

A vision for dignity without assimilation.

(3)

THE GOVERNMENT
The Betrayer of the Masses

The government's latest tactic is to ensure its dirty work is carried out without appearing directly involved. It increasingly relies on members of the community to implement its decisions, allowing the final framework to be enforced by others while the government remains hidden behind the scenes.

In doing so, the government avoids responsibility for anything that goes wrong or fails to meet the wishes, hopes, and welfare of the people. It achieves its goals without being held accountable for the consequences of its actions. The government now hides itself more than ever, watching the damage unfold from behind glass windows while denying direct involvement, even though all decisions are its own and are carefully plotted and planned.

The government has drifted far from its traditional role of serving the people who elected it and placed it in power. Those people trusted that the government would honour the promises it made during elections and act in their best interests.

Traditionally, the role of government was to serve the people: to provide education, healthcare, employment opportunities, security, and protection, and to guarantee that society could live in justice and peace.

That was the dream people believed in when electing a government. But what is the reality today? What is the truth people wake up to after every election?

Soon after elections, people discover that they have elected corrupt liars—individuals who lie openly and publicly, fully aware that they will not be held accountable. There are no laws to punish them for deceiving the public or exploiting the poor and vulnerable. They continue unpunished until their damage becomes too obvious to ignore. By then, a new corrupt government takes over and continues the same work of victimising the innocent.

The victimisation of innocent people should be considered the greatest crime of all, given its devastating impact on the lives and futures of millions. Yet history shows that those who commit crimes against the innocent are rarely, if ever, brought to justice. That failure itself is the greatest crime.

At worst, when such criminals are exposed—usually because they failed to cover their tracks properly—they may be asked to resign. Often, they leave with generous payouts funded by the blood and sweat of the weak and vulnerable, who struggle daily just to survive.

Governments are elected to serve and protect the interests of the people. Instead, what do they do? They close schools, hospitals, police stations, factories, companies, and banks. They force people into unemployment and dependency on welfare systems that provide insecurity rather than support.

They sell banks and major companies that belong to the public. They reduce interest rates to encourage people to buy homes and vehicles, and once borrowing reaches its limit, they raise interest rates sharply. At that point, families can no longer meet their repayments. The same corrupt government then seizes back homes and cars, destroying the lives and hopes of thousands of families.

Social Services, Privatisation, and Economic Control

All governments seem to do is play games, convinced of their superiority over the people they govern. They know that ordinary people are largely powerless and unable to effect real change. In most cases, by the time the pain and suffering become visible, the damage has already been done. Lives are lost, families are destroyed, homes are broken, and children are driven onto the streets to survive by any means possible.

How many times has the government ever listened to the cries of the people? How often has it changed its plans because citizens objected to the closure of a hospital, a school, or a police station? How many times has the government responded to demands to reduce fuel prices or stop increases in public transport fares?

Every one of these increases is money taken from the blood and sweat of poor, vulnerable, and innocent people. It is a crime when a working person earning fifty dollars a day must spend ten to fifteen dollars simply to travel to and from work.

Yet the greatest crime of all is the introduction of the Goods and Services Tax (GST)—a tax that no one in this country wanted. Despite widespread opposition, the corrupt and deceitful government imposed it anyway. I hope to live to see the day when the Prime

Minister responsible for inflicting this crime on the people is brought to justice.
And what of the opposition, waiting for its turn at the next election? They are pleased that someone else has already done the dirty work. They are happy to blame the previous government while quietly continuing the same policies themselves.
People elect governments to work for them, not against them. To give, not to take away. To allow people to live in peace, not fear. To protect citizens, not to allow criminals to roam freely, attacking innocent and vulnerable families, stealing the small possessions and hard-earned savings that took years to accumulate.
A government should never be a profit-making organisation. Its purpose is not to generate revenue at any cost. Yet modern governments do exactly that, regardless of the human toll, even if it means walking over dead bodies.
Privatisation is one of the greatest crimes committed by governments against the people. It involves selling assets that belong to the public without public consent. It is the theft of collective wealth, carried out under the false pretence of efficiency and reform.
These changes are serious, and people must become aware of what is happening before it is too late.
The government plans and implements sweeping changes—particularly in education—designed to deprive vulnerable members of society of opportunity. It no longer believes everyone is worthy of education. It claims that some students are not interested in learning and therefore do not deserve investment.

To justify this, the government deliberately undermines public education. It appoints poorly qualified teachers, many of whom struggle with the language of instruction. It creates hostile working conditions, provides unsuitable learning environments, overloads teachers with administrative tasks, and denies them time to teach effectively or monitor student progress.

Absent teachers are rarely replaced. Classes are merged, forcing one teacher to manage fifty or sixty students at once, reducing education to little more than crowd control. Teachers become exhausted and ill, leading to further absences and a downward spiral of failure.

Rules governing teacher employment are constantly changed to place educators under tighter government control. Teachers are expected to obey instructions without question. Any resistance can lead to dismissal under newly introduced legal frameworks that prevent meaningful challenge or appeal.

This places teachers at the mercy of the government—and students, in turn, at the mercy of teachers. A student's future is no longer determined by ability alone, but by compliance and favour.

Education, Control, and the Destruction of Student Futures

Under the new education system, teachers are given extensive control over students and their futures. Final outcomes are no longer determined solely by external examinations, which once provided a fair and uniform measure of ability. Instead, results are divided between final exams and assessments completed throughout the school year.

Under the old system, any student—regardless of background, nationality, race, or religion—who performed well in a final external examination could choose their preferred course of higher education or university. That system limited government interference and ensured that talent and effort were the decisive factors.

That system no longer exists.

By incorporating year-long assessments into final results, students are placed under the direct control of teachers, who themselves are under the control of the government. A teacher's judgment—whether fair or not—can now permanently damage a student's future. A single unjust or biased assessment can erase years of effort and destroy a student's prospects entirely.

Repeating a year does not fix the problem. It merely repeats the outcome. Teachers rarely change their assessment decisions, regardless of how much effort a student makes or how many times the year is repeated. Once a student has been marked down, their fate is effectively sealed.

This system allows the government to determine who may advance into professions such as medicine, law, engineering, or academia, and who will be excluded. It enables authorities to decide who will serve the system and who will be discarded by it.

Students are categorised, controlled, and filtered. Those deemed undesirable are quietly pushed out of the education system altogether. Public school teachers are often instructed to teach the same limited material repeatedly, term after term, year after year, deliberately boring students and encouraging them to leave.

Each student who drops out represents a financial saving for the government.

Parents, once the primary decision-makers in their children's futures, have been stripped of their authority. They no longer have a meaningful voice in educational outcomes. Their children—once their greatest hope—are subjected to systems that operate without transparency or accountability.

Parents watch helplessly as their children's futures are dismantled. Dreams are crushed, ambitions destroyed, and young lives redirected into paths they did not choose.

The government has effectively replaced parents. It claims ownership over students' lives and futures, conditioning them to accept government authority as absolute and unquestionable.

The system works tirelessly to separate children from their parents, convincing students that the government knows what is best for them, even if that means denying them access to higher education. Parents are portrayed as obstacles, their ambitions labelled harmful or unrealistic.

Students are indoctrinated to believe that their parents are responsible for their failures. Retaliation is redirected inward—towards families—while the system itself remains untouchable.

Certain groups can be singled out, isolated, and eliminated from professional pathways altogether. By controlling educational outcomes, the system ensures that entire communities are prevented from advancing, reproducing cycles of disadvantage across generations.

Children are vulnerable, impressionable, and easily manipulated. Schools operate with carefully designed structures, long-term planning, and clearly defined objectives. Parents, by contrast, often struggle without institutional support, attempting to counter years of daily conditioning.

Over time, many parents are forced to accept a painful truth: the system has shaped their children more powerfully than they ever could. Their children are no longer their own—they are products of the system.

Justice, Policing, and the Criminalisation of Victims

The education system is not the only structure under total government control. The same hierarchy and methods operate across every other public system, including policing and justice. While authorities claim these systems are "safe and sound," reality shows otherwise.

Under the current justice system, criminals are routinely set free to commit further crimes—particularly when they belong to protected families or influential groups. Ordinary people, by contrast, have little to no access to justice when they need it most.

Many victims make it as far as a lawyer's office, only to be turned away when confronted with unaffordable legal fees. Faced with the demand for large upfront payments before any action can be taken, they leave defeated—often in tears. Their pain is not only from what happened to them, but from what did not happen: justice.

Most victims are forced to accept their victimhood. They endure abuse, theft, and violence with no realistic path to accountability or protection.
How many people leave a courtroom believing justice has been served? Try to find one. More often, victims exit courtrooms shattered, having been victimised again—this time by a legal system that claims to defend them.
While victims leave in tears, criminals often leave with smiles. The true winners, however, are the lawyers—those who profit regardless of truth, guilt, or innocence.
Under this injustice system, victims may stand inside their own homes and watch intruders steal their belongings—items earned through years of hard work, sacrifice, and struggle. They can do nothing to stop it. Many no longer even bother calling the police, particularly if they have experienced indifference or hostility before.
Beyond financial loss, such crimes represent an invasion of privacy, dignity, and family life. For parents, especially, the experience is deeply traumatising. To watch thieves steal from your home while knowing that defending yourself could result in your own arrest is a devastating reality.
Children who witness such incidents carry that trauma for life. They grow up in fear, learning early that justice does not protect the innocent.
The most disturbing realisation is that these crimes happen constantly, and the system offers no meaningful deterrent. Certain groups are expected to be victims. The question is never *whether* someone will suffer, but *who*.

If a victim attempts to defend themselves, they are no longer treated as victims. They become criminals in the eyes of the law. The intruder becomes protected, while the homeowner risks prosecution, imprisonment, and permanent criminal records.
People learn quickly what the system expects of them: raise your hands, submit, and hope for survival. Resistance is punished. Compliance is enforced.
Under this system, criminals have rights. Victims do not. What kind of justice is that?
The deterrence that once protected communities no longer exists. Thieves are arrested and released within hours, allowed to return to the same neighbourhoods and target the same homes. Stolen property is rarely recovered. The risk to criminals is minimal; the reward is substantial.
Victims are left to suffer in silence, knowing that reporting crimes often leads to more harm than help.

Elections, Democracy, and the Illusion of Choice

Elections are the greatest illusion of the Western political system. If voting were not compulsory, most people would never attend on election day. That alone would reveal how little faith the public has in those seeking to govern them.
Compulsory voting hides the truth. People are forced to attend under threat of fines. They arrive unwillingly, disillusioned, and detached. Faced with a list of unfamiliar names and empty promises, many simply choose the least objectionable option, not because they believe in it, but because they are required to select someone.

If politicians truly wanted to know how popular they were, they would make voting voluntary. Only then would election results reflect genuine public support. Those who believe in a party or a candidate would attend voluntarily. Those who do not would stay away. If no one turned up to vote, it would be undeniable proof that none of the candidates deserved to govern. It would expose widespread distrust, dissatisfaction, and rejection of the entire political class.

Supporters argue that people can attend elections and vote against all candidates. In reality, such votes are meaningless. A rejection vote is quietly redistributed in favour of one party or another, with no transparency and no accountability. There is no way to verify where such votes ultimately end up.

The true objective is to bring as many people as possible to the polling stations. Once there, votes can be manipulated, redirected, or neutralised according to predetermined outcomes. Political deals are often made in advance—this term is yours, the next is mine. To major parties, government and opposition are merely alternating roles within the same system.

Opposition parties benefit from losing. They avoid responsibility while maintaining visibility, appearing in the media just enough to remain relevant until the next election cycle.

If no one voted, manipulation would be impossible. There would be no figures to alter, no ballots to replace, and no numbers to adjust. That is precisely why voting is compulsory—to conceal the rot at the core of the so-called democratic system.

What happens to ballot boxes after polling closes? Who transports them? Who supervises them? The public is asked to trust systems that operate without transparency. Physical ballots can be replaced. Digital systems can be programmed to add, remove, or redistribute votes at will.

Modern elections rely heavily on computerised counting systems—systems that can be altered silently and efficiently. Numbers can be adjusted to elevate one party and diminish another until the desired result is achieved.

Recent elections have demonstrated a new tactic: outcomes are left undecided until the final moments. This allows those controlling the process to evaluate which party is most willing to comply with instructions and offer concessions in exchange for victory.

Those who help governments come to power remain invisible. They operate behind the scenes, issuing demands that newly elected leaders must fulfil. Often, these demands involve decisions that harm ordinary people but serve larger strategic interests.

Immediately after close elections, governments frequently commit acts that betray the public. These actions were promised in private, exchanged for electoral victory, and carried out without public consent.

Thus, elections no longer determine policy. They merely determine which individuals will carry out decisions already made.

Foreign Influence, Media Coordination, and Controlled Leadership

Government control does not operate in isolation. State governments do not act independently, and national governments do not act alone. They are influenced, directed, and constrained by external forces that operate beyond public visibility.

Foreign governments, international organisations, and powerful financial interests exert influence over domestic policy. Decisions presented as "national interests" are often the result of negotiations conducted behind closed doors, with outcomes decided long before the public is informed.

State governments function as administrative arms rather than autonomous authorities. Their role is to implement directives, not to question them. When state leaders deviate from the agreed script, they are swiftly removed—either through internal party mechanisms, media pressure, or sudden "scandals" that appear at convenient times.

Leadership changes are rarely organic. Premiers and prime ministers are replaced not because the public demands it, but because they have failed to comply with expectations. Their successors are pre-selected, positioned, and promoted as "fresh leadership," even though policy direction remains unchanged.

The media plays a central role in this process. News outlets do not investigate power; they manage perception. Narratives are coordinated across platforms, ensuring consistency in language, framing, and emphasis. Dissenting voices are marginalised, ridiculed, or silenced altogether.

When leadership changes occur, media coverage follows a predictable script: praise for the outgoing leader's "service," excitement about the incoming leader's "vision," and assurances that the transition represents renewal rather than continuity. The public is encouraged to believe that change has occurred, even when nothing of substance has altered.

Journalists who question these narratives are sidelined or removed. Editors learn quickly which stories are permitted and which are forbidden. Those who comply are rewarded with access, exclusives, and career advancement. Those who do not disappear.

Foreign policy decisions provide the clearest example of this coordination. Military involvement, trade agreements, and sanctions are framed as moral imperatives, even when they damage domestic industries and harm citizens. Debate is suppressed, and dissent is equated with disloyalty.

Public fear is a powerful tool. Crises—real or exaggerated—are used to justify emergency powers, rushed legislation, and the erosion of civil liberties. Once these powers are granted, they are rarely surrendered.

The public is told that sacrifices are necessary, temporary, and unavoidable. Yet those sacrifices are always borne by ordinary people, never by those issuing the directives.

Through media repetition and controlled messaging, the population is conditioned to accept outcomes they did not choose. Compliance is framed as responsibility. Obedience is framed as virtue.

In this environment, leadership is no longer about representation. It is about management. Elected officials serve as intermediaries between external power structures and the public, translating directives into domestic policy while shielding their true origins. The illusion of sovereignty remains intact only because the public is never allowed to see who is truly making the decisions.

Identity, Division, Fear, and the End Result

To maintain control, the system must keep people divided. Unity is dangerous; division is manageable. Society is therefore broken into categories—race, religion, gender, culture, ideology, and class—each encouraged to see the other as a threat.

People are taught to identify themselves not as citizens with shared interests, but as members of competing groups. Loyalty is redirected away from community and family and toward abstract identities promoted by the state and reinforced by the media.

Fear is the primary weapon. Fear of crime. Fear of poverty. Fear of social exclusion. Fear of being labelled, reported, or punished. Fear keeps people compliant and isolated. It discourages questioning and suppresses resistance.

Those who speak out are quickly discredited. They are labelled extremists, conspiracy theorists, or troublemakers. Their arguments are not addressed; their character is attacked. The goal is not to debate, but to silence.

Over time, people learn to self-censor. They weigh every word, every opinion, every conversation. Silence becomes a survival strategy. When enough people remain silent, control becomes effortless.

The long-term damage is profound. Trust between neighbours erodes. Families fracture. Communities collapse into suspicion and resentment. People retreat inward, focused on survival rather than cooperation or progress.

Children grow up in an environment where conformity is rewarded and independent thought is punished. They learn early that obedience is safer than honesty.

Creativity, curiosity, and dissent are treated as threats rather than strengths.

The result is a population that is educated but not enlightened, informed but not empowered, connected but not united. People are surrounded by information, yet deprived of truth.

What remains is a managed society—orderly on the surface, hollow beneath. Elections continue, schools operate, courts function, and media broadcasts daily. The appearance of normality is carefully maintained. But beneath that surface lies a population stripped of agency, dignity, and genuine choice.

This is not freedom. It is control refined, normalised, and disguised as protection.

And until people recognise it for what it is, the system will continue to function exactly as intended.

In Australia, historical records show that individuals who stood up for justice were often rounded up, interrogated, tortured, persecuted, and ultimately imprisoned for many years without due process of law. Today, dissenting voices are frequently labelled as hate speech, while silence is promoted as virtue—raising the question of whether this is democracy or dictatorship.

(4)

FATHER AND SON

When reading this chapter, even men will cry.

This young man was born and raised in an Islamic country, in a practising, elementary middle-class Muslim family. He himself never missed a prayer. His poor father struggled to send him to school and later to university. The son was devoted to his studies and hoped that, upon graduating, he could ease his father's burden of supporting the family.

He excelled in his postgraduate studies, and the government selected him to pursue a doctorate in a Western country. After four years abroad, he successfully completed his doctorate and returned home.

His elderly parents went to the airport to welcome him. The father later recalled standing behind the glass, watching his son—whom he had not seen for four years—step off the aeroplane.

The father said that the moment he saw his son, an unexplained fear settled in his heart. When the son approached, both parents moved forward to embrace him. The father stepped aside to allow the mother to hug her son first. As she opened her arms, the son gently pushed her away, signalling that he did not wish to be hugged.

The father later described this moment as deeply painful. He could only imagine the hurt his wife felt. Still, he chose silence, unwilling to upset his son after such a long separation. He reassured the mother by saying, *"Perhaps he is tired from the journey. Give him time to rest."*

The father later reflected that his son's gaze made them feel as though something about them was suddenly wrong—how they dressed, how they spoke, or something deeper that they could not immediately name.

A few hours later, the call to prayer echoed from the nearby mosque. The parents instinctively looked to their son, who showed no response. The father tried to excuse this by telling himself that exhaustion was the cause. He decided it was better not to invite his son to prayer than risk upsetting him.

After the parents finished praying, the son remarked, **"Do you still do these kinds of things?"**

The father recalled that this single sentence caused a flood of memories—from the moment his son was born, through years of sacrifice, hardship, and hope. He remembered giving up food for his child, celebrating his graduation, and the fear he felt sending him alone to the West.

His first thought was disbelief: *Is this really my son?*

The memories answered him: *Yes. He is my son.*

Yes, the child I carried in my arms.
Yes, the boy whose illness felt like my own.
Yes, the young man who wept before leaving home, unable to bear the thought of leaving his parents behind.

Before his departure, the son had asked, *"Dad, what advice do you give me before I go?"*

The father replied, *"Your name is Muhammad. Go as Muhammad, and return as Muhammad."*

The son returned—but soon began expressing dissatisfaction with his parents' modest home. The furniture, the simplicity, and the lifestyle no longer met his expectations as a Western-educated professional.

The very home that had witnessed his childhood—where his mother once knelt to clean after him—now felt, to him, unsuitable.

He eventually chose to move out, distancing himself from his parents' religious practices and way of life. He later sought opportunities to return permanently to the West.

The father reflected that when his son was young, he feared losing him to illness or death. He did not lose him to death, but to what he perceived as a profound ideological transformation.

From this perspective, the father believed that cultural and ideological influence can sometimes have deeper and longer-lasting effects than military conflict, with consequences that extend across generations.

He wondered what kind of family his son would now build, what values would be passed on, and whether the sacrifices once made for him would be repeated for his own children.

In the father's view, Islamic teachings emphasise responsibility, care, restraint, and accountability in raising children. He questioned whether these values could survive after what he saw as a fundamental shift in belief and lifestyle.

The father viewed Western culture as operating under man-made systems that, in his opinion, weaken traditional family structures and moral boundaries. From his standpoint, these systems often promote values that conflict with Islamic teachings.

He feared that his son would feel compelled to conform to social norms—mixed-gender environments, entertainment culture, and educational systems—that the father believed could undermine moral development.

The father believed the cost of material success—larger homes, status, and wealth—had come at the price of faith, identity, and family unity.

He stated that if his son had died abroad, he could have accepted it as fate, but the transformation he witnessed upon his return caused him far greater pain.

From this viewpoint, ideological conversion is seen as more effective for Western influence than direct conflict.

The father believed that modern cultural influence operates subtly—entering homes, shaping values, and altering identities over time.

In his analysis, Islam is not confronted openly, but gradually diluted through media, education, and lifestyle norms. He believed that faith is not removed outright, but reshaped into a form that no longer governs daily life.

The father viewed Western media and education systems as powerful tools that influence behaviour, values, and aspirations, particularly among young people.

He believed that economic dependence, cultural imitation, and political pressure reinforce this

influence, creating long-term reliance rather than independence.
From his perspective, historical colonisation and modern global systems have left many Muslim societies dependent on Western institutions, markets, and governance models.
The father believed that this dependency extends to food, clothing, entertainment, education, and even political leadership.
In his view, the ultimate aim of this influence is to redirect loyalty—from spiritual foundations to worldly systems.
He concluded that the conflict is not merely political, but cultural and ideological: a struggle between two worldviews.
The father believed that Islamic culture does not seek to eliminate other cultures, but insists on its own moral and spiritual authority for those who choose it.
He argued that misunderstanding this distinction has fuelled decades of conflict.
In his final reflection, the father maintained that faith, once fully internalised, cannot be destroyed—but it can be weakened when detached from daily life.

(5)

ISLAM IN THE WEST
Understanding Islam on its own terms

Living in what is commonly referred to as the West, a fundamental question is often raised: *Who are you?* The answer frequently given is that the West represents a political, economic, and cultural system. Critics of this system argue that, historically, the shaping and manipulation of political opinion have been among its primary tools for extending influence over countries and states.

According to these critics, global influence depends on subjecting populations to a particular agenda and neutralising opposition. They argue that the greatest perceived threat to this agenda is not military force or legal authority, but independent and free-thinking minds. From this perspective, efforts to expand surveillance, regulation, and technological oversight are viewed as attempts to exert control over many aspects of human life.

It is further argued that international financial institutions, dominated by Western powers, exert pressure on developing nations through economic leverage. Critics claim that states which do not comply with expected policies face severe financial consequences, leading to long-term hardship for their populations.

Some commentators also argue that Western policies have treated human lives as expendable in the pursuit of strategic goals. They point to allegations—contested and widely debated—that certain diseases originated in military or experimental contexts, and that vulnerable populations were affected through unethical practices. These claims remain matters of controversy and belief rather than established fact, yet they continue to shape distrust toward Western institutions among many communities.

From a religious perspective, some believers hold that modern secular systems attempt to replace divine authority with human-made laws, presenting themselves as the ultimate source of justice. In this view, technology is perceived as a means of constant monitoring, and scientific advances such as genetics are sometimes interpreted as efforts to alter creation itself. Critics see this as an expression of arrogance, where only self-defined rules are recognised.

Within Islamic tradition, there are narrations attributed to the Prophet Muhammad describing times of widespread confusion, where truth is rejected and falsehood accepted, and where those distant from divine guidance gain influence. Many believers interpret contemporary global politics—such as gatherings of nations at international institutions—as fitting within this broader spiritual narrative, though such interpretations remain matters of faith.

Critics within Muslim communities argue that material wealth, consumerism, and the pursuit of pleasure have drawn many people away from religious principles. They describe this as a poor exchange, believing that periods of hardship reveal sincerity of faith. Some Muslims, it is argued, have adopted Western lifestyles while retaining only outward symbols of religious identity, embracing systems they believe have historically harmed Muslim populations through political inaction or selective intervention in places such as Bosnia, Kashmir, and Kosovo.

From this viewpoint, adherence to secular systems while rejecting divine law is seen as a spiritual contradiction. Those who hold this belief warn of moral accountability in the hereafter, framing their critique as theological rather than political.

Power, Control, and Security

Critics argue that Western influence operates both directly, through military and economic measures, and indirectly, through ideological means. They believe that unity among Muslims and a revival of religious principles are viewed as threats to global dominance, and that many policies are designed to prevent such unity.

Some observers claim that rising crime rates, drug distribution, and public insecurity are tolerated or inadequately addressed in order to justify expanded surveillance and policing powers. According to this argument, fear becomes a tool for increasing control.

Advances in technology—data collection, monitoring, and predictive analytics—are seen as mechanisms for influencing behaviour rather than simply maintaining order.

In this critique, personal choice within Western societies is described as limited, shaped by information control and social conditioning. Media narratives highlighting violence and insecurity are believed to create public acceptance of intrusive security measures, further expanding state authority. Concerns are also raised about large-scale data collection systems, identity databases, and tracking technologies. Critics argue that such systems enable detailed profiling of individuals, making populations easier to predict and influence. Whether viewed as protection or intrusion, these developments are central to debates about freedom and privacy.

International Institutions and Conflict

Some commentators claim that international organisations, particularly those influenced by Western powers, operate selectively. They cite historical events where peacekeeping forces allegedly failed to prevent mass civilian suffering, or where military action resulted in widespread destruction. These claims are often framed as moral criticisms rather than legal conclusions.

After the Cold War, many believed that Western systems had emerged without serious opposition. However, critics argue that ongoing injustice and environmental degradation have generated resistance rooted in religious and moral identity. Islam, in particular, is viewed by some believers as a system that cannot be absorbed into secular global structures.

The Gulf War is often cited as an example of media-driven conflict, where narratives emphasised military superiority while obscuring political motivations. Some argue that regional governments functioned within broader strategic frameworks determined by powerful states. The war is described by critics as a

catalyst for long-term military presence in the Middle East, especially in areas of religious significance.
Health issues affecting veterans of the Gulf War are frequently raised in discussions about accountability. While causes remain contested, questions persist regarding exposure to experimental treatments or environmental hazards. These concerns extend beyond any single nation and reflect broader anxieties about the treatment of soldiers.

Wealth, Media, and Cultural Influence
A recurring argument is that control of natural resources—particularly oil—is essential to Western economic stability. Critics believe that political influence over resource-rich Muslim countries is maintained through compliant leadership and economic dependency.
Media is also viewed as a powerful cultural instrument. Films, television, and music are described as vehicles for shaping perceptions and marginalising religious values. From this standpoint, Islam is often portrayed negatively, while secular identities are promoted as superior.
Australia, as a Western nation, is included in these critiques due to its participation in international conflicts. Some believers argue that continued military involvement contributes to global instability rather than peace. Others frame these developments as part of a broader historical cycle, believing that moral decline accelerates religious revival.

Faith, Law, and Moral Order
Many religious critics argue that a just global order cannot be achieved through systems disconnected

from divine guidance. They reject the idea that moral authority can emerge from leaders whose personal conduct is seen as flawed. From this perspective, only a system grounded in divine law can establish lasting justice.

Some argue that attempts to reinterpret Islamic teachings to align with modern secular norms undermine the integrity of the religion. Debates around issues such as modest dress, criminal law, and moral boundaries are viewed by traditional scholars as efforts to dilute religious principles. These internal debates are intense and ongoing within Muslim communities.

Critics of reformist approaches argue that Islam does not require reinterpretation to remain relevant, asserting that its principles are timeless. They emphasise that preservation of faith is understood, within theology, as a divine responsibility rather than a human one.

Purpose, Life, and Accountability

Islamic belief frames life as preparation for accountability after death. Material success, from this viewpoint, is not the measure of achievement. Critics of Western philosophy contrast this with what they perceive as a culture focused on consumption and immediate gratification.

Supporters of this critique often point to social issues—such as loneliness, mental health struggles, and suicide—as evidence that material comfort does not guarantee fulfilment. They argue that true contentment arises from submission to divine guidance rather than accumulation of wealth.

Islam presents itself, in this belief system, as a comprehensive way of life governing personal conduct, social relations, and moral responsibility. Adherents argue that religious commandments aim to protect human dignity and social harmony, while secular systems prioritise individual desire.

Conclusion

From the perspective presented here, the tension between Islam and Western systems is understood as a struggle between differing moral frameworks. This critique views Western dominance as rooted in power rather than justice, and Islam as offering an alternative grounded in accountability to God.

This manuscript represents **belief, interpretation, and critique**, not calls for harm or hostility toward individuals or peoples. Its central appeal is for reflection on morality, justice, and the purpose of human existence.

(6)

THE MEDIA
The One-Eye Approach

In today's world, whenever the word *media* is mentioned, the word most commonly associated with it by many thoughtful observers is *hypocrisy*.

Many people believe that media is not merely a channel of information, but a mechanism through which messages are repeatedly delivered until they take permanent residence in the mind. No matter how much one initially resists, rejects, or questions these messages, the constant repetition often leads to eventual acceptance. Over time, resistance gives way to exhaustion, and doubt is replaced by conformity. The impact of such messaging can be long-lasting.

The media, as an institution, does not stop delivering narratives it considers important. Critics argue that it relies on repetition as a method of persuasion, continuously reinforcing particular viewpoints until alternative interpretations are marginalised or forgotten. At that stage, the individual no longer challenges the message, but instead accepts and supports it.

Many commentators regard the media as one of the most powerful tools ever created for influencing public opinion. It provides a structure through which

dominant narratives can be maintained with remarkable resilience.
Some critics describe global power structures as being divided between those who benefit from influence and those who are subjected to it. From this perspective, the media is seen as a tool designed primarily to serve the interests of those in power, rather than the public at large.
From early on, those who control major institutions appear to have understood the importance of shaping opinion. To influence how people think, one must influence the information they receive. When messages are delivered simultaneously to large populations through unified platforms, acceptance becomes easier, as individuals assume that others agree with what is being presented.
When millions receive the same narrative, it begins to resemble an official truth—something that must be accepted rather than questioned. Over time, this repetition grants such narratives an authority similar to laws or social norms.
The media has become embedded in everyday life. Regardless of how busy people are, time is always found for news, screens, and updates. Many individuals rely on media as their primary source of information about the world, trusting that what they are told is accurate.
When the media reports an event occurring thousands of miles away, few question it. Trust has been built over decades, and with it, dependence. As a result, many people rarely challenge the framing, emphasis, or omissions within media reporting.
While much of the information conveyed may be factual, critics argue that the real concern lies in the

selection of stories, sources, and perspectives. Media outlets often rely on external institutions for information, some of which may have political, economic, or strategic interests.

In some cases, media organisations are accused of presenting information they know to be incomplete or misleading. In other cases, journalists may be persuaded that altering the presentation of facts is necessary to preserve social order, national interest, or stability. Under such reasoning, accuracy becomes secondary to perceived necessity.

Governments and authorities may instruct media outlets on how certain events should be reported, particularly when issues of national security, war, or foreign policy are involved. Journalists working within large institutions are often trained to follow editorial direction. Those who refuse risk losing their positions and careers.

In such environments, compliance becomes the norm. Even when individuals disagree, they may conclude that resistance is futile, as dissent rarely changes outcomes and often results in personal loss. Critics argue that this system encourages conformity and suppresses independent thought.

From this perspective, the narratives delivered to the public reflect the priorities of those who hold power. Media messaging can influence behaviour, voting patterns, and public attitudes, guiding societies in predetermined directions.

Some observers question whether it is truly possible to establish independent media under such conditions. Across different countries and languages, media systems often appear strikingly similar in structure, tone, and ideological alignment.

When influential groups decide to promote a particular individual, critics argue that media coverage can manufacture popularity. Through repeated positive exposure, the public is persuaded that a candidate is inevitable, competent, and widely supported—sometimes even before elections take place.

Conversely, leaders who challenge dominant interests may quickly be portrayed as corrupt, incompetent, or unpopular. Media narratives can shift rapidly, transforming public perception regardless of actual public support. Allegations are repeated until they are accepted as truth.

In this way, critics argue that the media can remove or elevate leaders without appearing to do so, maintaining the illusion of democratic choice while steering outcomes behind the scenes.

Within Western media environments, journalists are generally expected to operate within accepted ideological boundaries. Reporting that aligns with prevailing cultural, political, and strategic perspectives is rewarded, while dissenting views are marginalised or excluded.

Issues such as war, defence policy, and international relations are rarely presented with full transparency. Instead, reporting often reflects a single dominant perspective, leaving little room for alternative interpretations or uncomfortable truths.

Some observers argue that the realities of conflict zones are only partially reported. Civilian suffering may be acknowledged, but responsibility is rarely examined in depth. Investigations often stop short of challenging powerful actors.

Historical events involving large-scale civilian casualties continue to provoke debate, with critics questioning why accountability is applied selectively. They argue that some atrocities receive intense scrutiny, while others are minimised or justified.

The result, according to these critics, is a global information environment in which suffering is visible, but causes remain obscured. Responsibility becomes abstract, and outrage is carefully managed.

The same critics contend that media attention often arrives only after devastation has occurred, offering sympathy without accountability. This pattern, they argue, allows cycles of harm to continue without meaningful challenge.

In domestic affairs, media narratives are also said to prepare the public for political and economic changes. Shifts in leadership, policy, or social structure are often introduced gradually through messaging designed to normalise them.

Education systems, policing, employment, and public services are frequently portrayed as functioning well, even as many citizens experience declining conditions. Critics argue that this disconnect between lived reality and media portrayal deepens public frustration and mistrust.

Public education, in particular, is often praised in official narratives, while concerns raised by parents and educators are minimised. Some believe that systemic inequality is reinforced by an education system that favours wealth and social background over merit.

Private institutions, by contrast, are perceived as offering pathways unavailable to others, regardless of academic ability. From this viewpoint, opportunity is increasingly tied to ideology, social networks, and economic status.

Media coverage, critics argue, plays a key role in maintaining these perceptions. By promoting certain narratives and ignoring others, it helps preserve existing power structures while discouraging resistance.

Those who challenge dominant narratives—whether politicians, journalists, or public figures—may find themselves rapidly discredited. Media praise can turn to condemnation overnight, reinforcing the message that dissent carries consequences.

At the same time, media outlets enjoy considerable freedom when covering entertainment, fashion, sports, and celebrity culture. Critics argue that such content serves as distraction, filling space while serious issues remain under-examined.

Trends in behaviour, appearance, and lifestyle are often presented as personal choice, yet many believe these trends are carefully promoted. Repetition and social pressure create conformity, making deviation difficult.

From this perspective, people are encouraged to believe they are free while decisions are increasingly shaped for them—what to value, what to fear, and how to think about complex issues.

Ultimately, critics argue that the media operates with a "one-eye" approach—seeing only what power permits it to see. As long as this remains the case, public understanding will remain limited, and genuine accountability will remain elusive.

(7)

POLICE COUNTRY
The Ugly Force of Racism

It is quite often difficult to determine whether the police control the government or the government controls the police. In many situations, it appears that the government is in charge of the police. In other cases, the police have rounded up members of the government. One thing is certain: the police are there to protect the government and its interests.

Most people in the community understand what the word *police* means. Individuals wearing blue uniforms, carrying guns around their waists, bending under trees or hiding around corners to carry out their favourite hobby of taking photos of moving objects. Almost all of them are uneducated, even the most senior ones. They possess enormous amounts of hatred, rudeness, impoliteness, and impatience toward members of the community. They are overly eager to demonstrate how little authority they have and to prove that they are in control of any situation—often by flexing their muscles and using force against vulnerable individuals,

throwing people to the ground, twisting their arms, and sometimes breaking them. They handcuff people, rendering them motionless, speechless, and rightless. Some cannot stop themselves from delivering an extra blow to the heads of those they arrest, allegedly to prevent them from thinking clearly, so that when complaints are made, the victims cannot recall what truly happened. Most people who have dealt with the police have attempted to complain about them, only to realise that those who investigate the police are often more criminal than the police themselves.

Most of the time, they arrest people for no reason other than the fact that those people showed them that they are the most hated human beings on earth. Then they inform you of your rights, while the truth is that once you are in their hands, you have none.

They are above the law, and 99% of the time they get away with murder. If they are ever caught red-handed and brought before a judge, and if that judge feels unable to simply let them off, they may end up receiving a fine or being stood down for a few days—or even a few hours. Even this is rarely implemented or enforced, and the final result is that nothing happens to them, even when they are guilty of murder.

In the rare cases where the "wrong" judge presides and a police officer is convicted, the commissioner appeals on their behalf and ensures that the "right" judge hears the case, guaranteeing that their man will walk free. Not only does the commissioner get his man off, but the party that originally won the case may be forced to pay costs and suffer disruption after a total reversal of justice. The commissioner will never allow one of his men to go to prison, because doing so could expose other crimes and cause everyone to turn on one another—especially on their godfather, the commissioner himself.

This is a total abuse of justice—or perhaps the injustice system—carried out openly and publicly. The corrupted, one-eyed media narrates the story according to the commissioner's wishes. Even when all evidence points toward police wrongdoing, the media remains supportive, defending the police so that public confidence in the police force is not lost.

If you have dealt with the police even once, your impression of them will likely be very different from what you read in newspapers or see in television advertisements urging you to contact the police if you need help. The real experience is far removed from the false advertising for which this country is famous. You learn many facts about the police once you enter their premises. You learn that the police are the real criminals in this country. They are the ones who initiate, encourage, motivate, and participate in almost every crime that occurs in society. No crime is ever committed without their knowledge, approval, or assistance.

They are the ones who shoot innocent people. They either deal drugs themselves or take commissions from drug dealers. No drugs enter this country without their permission or approval. Many of them take payments from women who sell their bodies on the streets. They are involved in—and stand behind—every crime imaginable.

They drive around with sirens and lights on, coming from nowhere and going nowhere, simply to remind people that the police exist. Yet when people truly need them, they are never there. If they are present, they hide behind glass windows, watching you while remaining unseen. If you insist on seeing them and are willing to wait, one may emerge to tell you they are busy and that you should return another day, week, or even year to report your burglary or stolen car because they are understaffed. It is never their intention to disturb thieves or spoil their fun.

When they stop you for an alleged traffic offence you never committed—and they know you did nothing wrong—if they feel they may have difficulty proving it, or fear a complaint or witnesses, they may let you go. But only after convincing you that you were still in the wrong and that they are generously letting you off this time. This occasional act is done to improve their public image, but only when enforcement would be inconvenient. A bit of brainwashing from time to time is considered necessary, as long as it does not significantly affect revenue.

Anyone who has dealt with them realises that the last thing the police want to do is investigate crime. Often, they are connected to crimes themselves. It would be illogical for them to investigate their own actions. When forced to investigate, they simply find another suspect—often an innocent person who has nothing to do with this particular crime,—to balance their books and close the case.

Their attitude reveals one fact: crime is acceptable to them, and preventing it is not their role. Their true job becomes clear when they stop you for not wearing a seatbelt, failing to indicate, or driving 50 km/h in a 60 km/h zone. Thousands of people are falsely accused daily of speeding when they were nowhere near doing so. It is their word against yours, causing you to doubt even your own speedometer.

Their real purpose is also revealed on trains, where groups of officers target specific racial groups under the guise of ticket inspections—despite rail authorities having their own staff. I once witnessed twelve officers surround a single person who allegedly did not have a ticket. They stripped him of his clothes, shoes, and socks in public, even though he claimed he had purchased a ticket and was willing to buy another. The purpose was never fare enforcement; it was intimidation and control.

Police officers are paid danger allowances to check train tickets—justified as long as it generates revenue for the government. Crime prevention is never their concern. Their commissioner protects them, overturns convictions, and ensures loyalty. In return, officers collect revenue for political allies. Everyone benefits except the public.

They are the kind of people who would lie in front of you without shame. They would change what they said to you, or what you said to them a little while ago, without any regard or any concern, to anyone or anything, as long as it would suit them, and serve their purpose. It has to be their way and nothing else, even if they have to lie. 100 % of the time, if you try to put an opinion or a point of view to defend yourself, you would be threatened that you will be arrested and locked up. Those kinds of threats they make, most of the time, get people to keep quiet and not to say one more word, and usually frighten people. Who would want to be locked up in a cell and remain under the mercy of some wild and vicious animals, who follow no rules and obey no laws? Especially if they can rely on their commissioner and count on him to get the rope around their necks, if they were convicted of committing a murder.

They make themselves visible during rush hours to reinforce the illusion of safety, while victims of real crimes are told there is no one available to help. Ask where the police are, and you will be told anywhere except where crime occurs.

Who can speak well of them? Only hypocrites. They are among the most hated people in the community. Many avert their gaze when police are nearby, feeling fear or disgust.

They lie without shame, change their stories without concern, and threaten arrest whenever someone attempts to defend themselves. Such threats silence people through fear. Who would want to be locked in a cell under the control of violent individuals who obey no laws, knowing their commissioner will protect them even if they kill?

If the police wanted to stop drugs, they could do so within 24 hours. Children know where to buy drugs—yet police claim ignorance. Drug busts occur only when smugglers fail to involve police or refuse to pay. Drugs are allowed as long as “taxes” are paid. When disputes arise, the police orchestrate raids, invite the media, confiscate drugs, resell them, and collect praise.

The Western system ensures no one is held accountable. Lawyers protect lawyers, doctors protect doctors, judges protect judges, and police protect police. Truth is buried.

As you read this, criminals roam free while victims suffer beside the ugly face of justice. Justice has long been absent from the Western system. Victims lose rights daily until they feel forced to defend themselves. The law protects criminals, not victims. No victim ever finds true justice through the legal system. If all victims were asked whether they received justice, none would raise their hands.

People cry out for justice, yet do not know where to find it. Corrupted police, lawyers, judges, and politicians form a single criminal system. People avoid the police, fearing false accusations. Many do not report crimes to avoid encountering them.
Inside police premises, you are treated as a criminal. Officers search your history for faults to dismiss your complaint. The widespread comparison of police to pigs exists for a reason. Pigs thrive in filth—and so do police environments. There is no such thing as a clean police officer.
The title alone is sufficient. Everything else is merely a record of a continuous cover-up by government and police of crimes committed against the community.

A Justice System Without Justice

A justice system that is incapable of holding criminal police accountable for the killing of innocent people has forfeited its moral authority to exist.
It is catastrophic, shattering, and appalling to subject victims to the illusion that their rights will be upheld if they pursue justice in cases involving police or other government entities, when the outcome is effectively known before proceedings even begin. In such cases, victims are denied any genuine chance of success. The justice system, as it currently operates, appears designed to prevent accountability rather than deliver justice.
When the justice system of any society becomes unfair, oppressive, and tyrannical, it is a sign that the moral foundation of that society is eroding—and that its decline is inevitable.
I have not come across any information indicating that the Judicial Commission of New South Wales

has ever found a judge guilty of misconduct or bias, let alone referred a judge to Parliament for disciplinary action.

The justice system in this country continues to present a shocking display of its failure to hold criminal police accountable for any crime.

(8)

THE HIJAB
The Uniform of The Muslim Woman

The dignity, the honour, the respect, the morality of the Muslim woman in her Hijab. The wearing of the Hijab is the biggest, strongest and most effective way to represent Islam. For that, it is the most challenging rule of Islam that the disbelievers are trying to remove, or at least modify, to minimize its fiery effects. The Hijab of the Muslim woman is at the top of the disbelievers' most wanted list. It is considered by them to be a highly explosive, fiery weapon, a dangerous material, courageously outspoken, and a strong invitation designed completely and comprehensively to defy the whole world.

Year after year, generation after generation, the West, as well as some of the so-called Muslim thinkers who have been educated in the West by the West for the West, and then returned home to tell their Muslim mothers and sisters to take off their Hijab. Why? Asked the Muslim mothers and sisters. Because it is freedom, civilization, Westernization, modernization, and sophistication. But the real truth is that Western women are jealous of the Hijab of the Muslim women, and many Western women converted to Islam because they wanted to wear the Hijab. Western women are made to feel very cheap when standing next to a Muslim woman. The Hijab of the Muslim woman speaks out so loud to the non-Muslim woman and says, Why are you exposing yourselves? Why is your hair showing, let alone your arms and legs? Why are you letting everyone have a look at those exposed parts of your body? Your body is your property. Why do you let everyone see for free, whether you agree or not, they still see. You are making yourself seen by those who deserve to see, and those who do not deserve to see. In Islam, a Muslim woman is not public property. She is a unique individual, a very special, and very private being who ought to be treated with respect and honour, not an object that you see in the window and go inside to buy her for a few moments then spit on her, and walk out (in many European countries women are displayed in glass windows of shops for men to see and buy).

Exposing your body is advertising it for anyone who wants to see.

People advertise when they want to sell. Who do you want to sell to? To anyone in the streets? Are you saying to anyone you meet in the street, Look at my hair, look at my arms, look at my legs? What is the logic behind a woman exposing herself to everyone? Would it not be more logical for her to expose herself only to someone who deserves to see her, someone she cares for, and has some entitlement with her, someone she granted, and gave permission to see of her that which is not granted and permitted to everyone else? Should not those exposed parts be more valuable and more precious than to give away to everyone?

Muslim women are called upon by the demoralized West to take off their Hijab under the name of freedom. The Muslim woman's real freedom is in her wearing the Hijab. Exposing your body is becoming a slave to your desires, and accordingly, a slave to everyone else who wishes to enslave you.

A Muslim woman, by wearing her Hijab, is telling the whole world she is a representative of the last religion that God ordained for all mankind, Islam. She is telling the whole world to think about this world and the world hereafter. She is telling the whole world, " Think, why am I doing this? Why am I wearing that? Think about heaven, think about hell, think about a creator who ordered me to dress like that, and I am fulfilling his commands because I am afraid of him, not from anyone else. To him she belongs, and to him she will return. She is telling everyone she has courage, she has dignity, she is honest with herself, and with her Lord. She is faithful to her creator who made her, and she is submitting to his order, which is of great benefit to her, and it is there to protect her, and to safeguard her against herself as well as against the others. She is saying to the whole world she is strong, she has control over herself, and over her desire. She has her own mind, her own determination. She is sure of what she is and who she is. She is telling the whole world she can be trusted, relied on, and put in charge after being in charge of herself first. She is saying to the whole world, she is a servant of her creator, not a servant for the creations, and being faithful to him, to herself, to her mother, to her father, to her brother, to her husband, and to the whole of her Islamic community. She is a good influence and a good example. She is telling the whole world she is a beautiful person, inside and outside. She is precious, she is valuable, she is dear, honoured and respectable. She is telling the whole world she is a Muslim woman, and she is proud of her Islam. She has faith, she has a belief, she has someone to answer to, she has respect for whom she worships, and she knows he is watching her wherever she may be. She is telling everyone that she is not concerned about this ending world, she is looking forward to an everlasting life in the hereafter, and she is eager to meet her creator with her head covered.

The Muslim woman is unique in every way. She was honoured by her creator when he ordered her to cover herself. The Prophet Muhammad said that when people point at a Muslim woman because she is covering her head, the Creator Himself answers on her behalf by saying I am a witness she is a believer. What an honour, what a blessing, what a gift from the creator to the Muslim woman. Allah (swt) likes to see the Muslim woman in her Hijab. The disbelievers and the party of Satan like her to expose herself. Muslim women who are not complying with this very clear order of Allah (swt) should immediately reconsider their position, ask themselves, who are they following? Where are they heading? This is a very serious issue. Muslim women who do not cover themselves in the manner described for them by Allah are declaring war against Allah? Can they afford to do that?

The wearing of the Hijab is an order from the creator to all Muslim women and girls when they are about to start their teenage years. Those women and girls who do not follow this clear instruction of God are committing a major sin and defying the will of God. Severe punishment is waiting for them. The significance of the Hijab lies deep beyond covering the head. The Hijab is a uniform for the Muslim woman that tells that she is a soldier in the army of Allah, and she, with all due respect, is there to carry out his commands and obey his instructions. The Hijab signifies what she is, and who she is. The Hijab serves as a protector, a shield against all evils, and all the desires of this world. The manner in which the Hijab should be worn is precisely described in the Koran. The West, through its fashion design establishments, and advertising machine propaganda, have tried so hard to change the shape and the manner in which the Hijab is worn, to spoil the connection, the devotion, and the sincerity of the Muslim woman she has towards her creator. The result is what we see today, of some Muslim women wearing Hijab Western style, which does not relate to the teachings and the instructions of the true faith of Islam. But just like everything else that is Islamic, the West must interfere in an attempt to spoil the relationship between the Muslims and their creator, so that the Muslims are deprived of the help, the support, and the victory promised to them by the creator when following the right path.

The West tells women, leave your home, leave your children, leave your husbands, go out to work, earn money, be your own boss, independent, free, in control of your own life, in charge of your own destiny, decide your own fate, you are clever, intelligent, educated. You have not been created to be tied to the kitchen sink; go out.

Islam tells Muslim women to stay at home, look after their husbands, their children, and their elderly parents. Islam considers bringing up a family to be one of the most noble tasks assigned to human beings, and the reward for that is equal to that of the men going to fight the enemy in the war. When the creator ordered Muslim women to remain at home, it was for the women's best interests; it was to protect and look after such precious creations of God. The creator has made Heaven under the feet of motherhood, and those who disobey their mothers, and their mothers are discontent with them, will never enter into paradise. What a status that Islam has given to women. What other faith gave such an honour to women? Women have a great status in Islam, and Islam did not see any good in women going out to work and competing with men, except in special circumstances that necessitate that to take place. It is quite evident that a great deal of the chaos that the world is facing today is due to women going out to work, leaving their real job unattended, resulting in breaking down the family unit, and sending kids to the streets to die there.

Islam demands that women seek knowledge, be educated, intelligent and intellectual to look after their families in the best possible way.

Under the Western system, women have been used and abused; they go out to work, and still have to come home and do the job that can never be done by anyone else except the mothers. Under the Western system, women are not free; they have no rights, no respect, they are salves to their desires, and the desires of all those around them who like to see women exposing themselves, and prostituting themselves for the enjoyment, and the pleasure of some faithless, Godless men. In Western culture, women are just objects or commodities that can be bought and sold. The Western system is quite uncaring, unjust, unfair, and unkind to women. It deprives women of all their rights, all their dignity, and all respect. Under the name of civilization, the Western system asked women to take off their clothes, lie naked on the beaches, and walk naked on the streets, while the truth is, being naked is against any kind of civilization; it is a sign of being primitive and uncivilized. Under the Western system, women are nothing but slaves, who would listen, obey, and follow without having any form of power to challenge, object, or reject what has been dictated to them.

Under the name freedom of choice, the West has given women the freedom to do whatever they like; it all comes down to personal freedom and personal choice, which stops at nothing and has no limits. Recently, they came up with the idea that even your religion is a personal choice, and no one has any power to force anyone to practice any religion, which means Muslims cannot force their children to practise Islam if the children do not want to do so. Matters that are less important than the issue of faith have no ground for debating as being a personal choice. You drink alcohol, or you don't, is a personal choice; you smoke drugs, or you don't, is a personal choice; you commit adultery, or you don't, is a personal choice; you expose yourself, or you don't, is a personal choice; you get married, or you don't, is a personal choice. It a personal choice to do any of these things, but it is not a personal choice to wear a Hijab, to cover up, to be moral, to be shy, to be decent, this is not allowed, not permissible, you will be discouraged, you will be challenged, you will be prevented, you will be fought, you will be undermined, you will be discriminated against, you will be considered inferior, looked down upon, uncivilised, and you are not free.

The West says everything is personal choice, you are free to do what you like with yourself, to yourself, and about yourself. No, says Islam. WE belong to our creator; he is the one who owns us all. We are his servants, he commands us, orders us, guides us, instructs us, and we live according to his instructions, not according to our own wishes and our own desires. We have no right to do anything to ourselves except in accordance with the instructions of our creator. We do not own ourselves, and therefore we are not entitled to do what we like to ourselves.

He made the rules, guiding us to everything that has a benefit for us, and preventing us from doing anything that would cause harm or grief to us.

The West says we do not belong to our creator, and we will not return to him.

The West wants Muslim women to consider the Hijab a historical issue, and it is time to leave it behind.

The issue of the Hijab is an issue that no one, Muslim or non-Muslim, should give an opinion on. It is a matter that has been decided by the creator, and it is not for an open discussion or a debate.

The war that has been declared against Muslim women is not the kind of war that uses missiles and smart bombs directed at the heads of the Muslim women to destroy their Hijabs, but it is the war of rock and roll, the Pop music, the disco, the movies, the Television, the war of Brandy and alcohol. When you see a Muslim woman not practising her religion, you know she has surrendered after being defeated in that war that was declared against her by the West.

The West sends its wolves to Muslim countries to stir up women about the Hijab. Why are your women covering up their faces? How can they breathe the air? Should we not give them the right to see the life around them? Why do you make them see everything dark in front of their eyes?

In a society where women are covering themselves up, a society that is quite content, well-balanced and living in peace, why is there a need to call upon the women of such a society to change their situation? Why is there a need to try to convince these women that they are oppressed, victimized, unhappy, denied their rights, treated unfairly, suffering, having a complex, living in pain, grieved, and exhausted? and encourage them to ask, Why are Western women allowed to dress in fashion, and you Muslim women are not? Why are Western women allowed to go out anytime they want, talk with whoever they want, laugh, giggle, shake hands, touch, dance, sleep, and you Muslim women are not?

The West's intention goes far beyond asking women to cast off their veils.

Have you ever heard anyone asking, Why am I healthy?

Why am I enjoying a good life? Why am I physically and mentally fit? How can I get sick? How can I be unhealthy? How can I be unfit? How can I be unhappy? Show me the way to destroy myself, the way to contract diseases, and live in pain and agony. This is exactly what they are asking Muslim women to say when they ask them to uncover their heads. It is an invitation to destruction to be sick, unhealthy, unfit and unhappy. It is an invitation to throw away their morality and their shyness to turn them into a cheap commodity to be bought and sold and made available to whoever wants it.

Obviously, those who call upon Muslim women to cast off their veils think they know better than the creator who ordered women to cover up. May God guide them before they die.

The famous incident of the two Moroccan-born French girls will always remain to show the real identity of the West, when the two girls attempted to wear the Hijab at school, and the whole of France stood up against them, until the orders came from the highest level in government to expel them from the school for wearing the Hijab. This is in France, the nation of freedom, where anyone can do whatever they like, but not wear the Hijab. The freedom to be immoral is allowed, but the freedom to be moral is not allowed. Could those two little teenage Muslim girls be right, and the whole of France, including its government, be wrong, about the issue of the Hijab? Many Muslim women are confused; this is a time of confusion; they do not know what is right and what is wrong, what is good and what is evil, who is with you and who is against you, who is your friend and who is your enemy.

Many Muslim women have deserted the true knowledge of the religion and the true teachings of the Prophet. Many were misled by the decorated lifestyle presented to them in glamorous, attractive and bright shiny colours. Life is art, sport, tourism, movies, Television, going out, dressing up, and taking off.

The West has tried to reach many Muslim women, penetrating their lives through the West's one-eyed media. Almost 24 hours a day, fashion, art, sport, music, movies, but the bleeding wounded women in Bosnia, and in Kosovo, may be presented for a few seconds if that, and only after the raping were done, and the slaughtering were carried out, and the children were dragged away, and the identity were removed, and the homes were destroyed, and the belongings were scattered. The media will show the wounded, raped women, and the loud-screaming orphans queuing up for a loaf of bread supplied by the criminals themselves. The truth would shy away from the horrors of those weeping and bleeding women and children.

Their homes were destroyed, without any explanation,

Their blood was shed without any justification,

Their children were taken away to the disbelieving nations

If they were to return one day to visit their homeland, they would only see the sad graves of their parents, who were willing to give every drop of their blood and died for Islam.

The children of Islam are being sold in Western nations, while many Muslims are running around playing and having fun, not minding to be absent from the scene, and slumbering in a false dream. The West believes that taking Muslim children to Western

nations is an honour for these children, a gift, a favour, a humanitarian act, after their mothers were raped and their fathers were slaughtered, and their homes were destroyed.
The West would not allow an Islamic system where women would wear the Hijab to be established in any European country. European women were made to lie naked on the beach, to expose themselves, to entertain, and to provide pleasure. For the West, European women wearing a Hijab is outrageous.
An Islamic community in Europe, with its own identity, its own law, its own rule? What next, the West will ask? An Islamic constitution? You hope, but never.
As the Koran says, they will continue to struggle against you until you leave your religion; they wish that you would become disbelievers like them, then you will be all the same. Heaven is waiting, the fire of hell is waiting, we are waiting, and they are also waiting to see where our place will be.
With wearing the Hijab comes the responsibility of speaking the truth, living the truth and being with the truth.

Many ruling governments in Muslim countries, such as Tunisia and Turkey, are so frightened of the Hijab that they forbid women and girls to wear it. One will ask how these governments, which are supposed to have great power, total control, and have, at their disposal, the armies, the police, and in many cases the CIA, feel threatened by a scarf that a weak woman wears?. Such governments claim that they have freedom and democratic systems, and to some extent, it is true; they allow individuals to wear anything they like, but not the Hijab. Why? Because the Hijab reminds them of what they are trying hard to forget, and pretend it is not there. It reminds them that there is a religion called Islam. It reminds them that there is a heaven and a hell, a day of judgment, an account, a deed, a reckoning, a death, a grave, an end, a will, a power, a creator, a God, a questioning, a belief, and a Law other than theirs that mankind should submit to, and follow. It reminds them of what is waiting for them. They know it, they feel it, they know it is coming soon or later, but for now, they do not want to be reminded of any of that, they just want to live for the moment forget all about later.

The message that Hijab sends out to them loudly is the last thing they want to see or hear. They will not forbid a woman to wear a bikini or walk half naked in the streets, but they will forbid her to wear a Hijab that covers her head. Some people get offended when they see the sight of a naked woman, but how can anyone be offended when seeing a woman who is covering herself? What is there to offend anyone?

These governments denied any girl who wears the Hijab the right to education. The Turkish government appointed special police to stand outside government schools, to prevent any girl who wears the Hijab from entering. At universities, women and girls who wore the Hijab were removed by force.

In Turkey again, a woman who wears a Hijab is not allowed to be employed by any government agency, and any other private establishment that dares to employ such a woman will risk it with the government. More Muslim countries started to put more restrictions on women wearing the Hijab, to discourage them from presenting themselves as Muslims. While all the Western-appointed puppet leaders ruling Muslim countries are making extensive and unprecedented efforts to stop Muslim women from wearing the Hijab, many Muslim women all over the world are too busy putting it back on.

The anti-Islamic Turkish government, which had made more effort in this field than any other Muslim government hoping to eliminate the sight of the Hijab in the Turkish society, trying to defy Allah, was shocked when one of the politicians turned up for her parliamentary duties wearing a full Hijab. Every member of the 550 representatives stood up, in a state of disbelief, to look at her, more precisely at her Hijab, which they had thought they had got rid of once and for all, and here it is, all of a sudden, turning up at the very foot steps of their parliament. The behaviour of the 550 members of parliament were astonishing, they all yelled out at once and would not keep quiet, or calm down until the Woman with the Hijab was sent out the parliament, they were relieved only when the sight of the Hijab disappeared, and they were no longer reminded of Islam, but the message was delivered by a very brave and gracious soldier of Allah, dressed in the uniform of the Muslim woman.

It may seem to some Muslim women that wearing the Hijab is inviting troubles, and as a result, it seems to some like being in hell, like the Turkish sister who sacrificed her parliament job, but kept her Hijab. On the other hand, it may seem that walking while exposing yourself is being free and seems like heaven.

The truth of the matter is, the hell of wearing the Hijab is the real heaven, and the heaven of being exposed is the real hell.

What is the secret behind this little scarf that Muslim women have been ordered by their creator to wear? Is it really capable of overthrowing governments? What are these governments afraid of? It is only a piece of material. What is so distinctive about the Hijab? These governments simply see the Hijab as a symbol of communalist identity.

Despite restrictions, criticism, or misunderstanding, and the efforts of those governments to forbid the wearing of the Hijab, the number of Muslim women choosing to wear the Hijab continues to grow globally. For many, it represents resilience, faith, and commitment in the face of pressure, challenging these governments, and sending out a loud message to them, that says this is your law, and this is God's law, which one is prevailing?

The Hijab remains, for believing Muslim women, a symbol of obedience to God, moral clarity, and spiritual dignity. Wearing it is understood as an act of worship, undertaken for the pleasure of Allah alone—not for social approval or acceptance.

(9)

GOVERNMENTS IN THE DARKNESS
The Preventers of the Light

When will the West face reality and recognise itself as an evil culture of wolves, and admit it? When will the West, for once, uncover and publicise the truth about the misuse of its power, the abuse of its authorities, the magnitude of its control, and the depth of its involvement in the victimisation of innocent human beings?

When will the West take off its mask and show its real identity—its real objectives, its real purpose, its real intentions, its real goals, its real ambitions, and its hypocrisy? What does it truly hope to achieve?

Why does the West create hunger and starvation, poverty and disease, while preventing the weak and innocent from accessing education and medical care, and then watch them die while waiting for Western-made medications? Why does the West halt economic growth and prevent the industrialisation of many nations?

The Western governments, almost without fail, insist on having everything their own way. The people have no real say. Under the West's so-called democratic system, people are convinced that they have the right to elect those who govern them. Accordingly, once a government is elected, people expect that their wishes, and the promises made to them, will be fulfilled.

However, once a Western government enters office, it stops serving—or even thinking about—those who elected it. Instead, its focus becomes how to remain in power and how to benefit from it personally. Western governments, once in office, often do the opposite of what they promised. They deliver the opposite of what people waited for, expected, and hoped the elected government would achieve on their behalf.

Over the years, people have learned never to expect what they were promised. They have learned to tolerate disappointment and to accept the fact that, once again, they have been deceived, cheated, misled, and betrayed by their own elected governments. All they can do is wait for the next election, only to be tricked again with new promises and new breaches of those promises.

People living under the Western system have been conditioned to accept deception by their elected governments. The West has succeeded in convincing people that waiting patiently for change is part of being civilised, when in truth it is part of being victimised.

Western governments have become governments that victimise people in a "civilised" manner, training the population to endure hardship while waiting for the next change of power.

What kind of civilised government refuses to listen to the wishes of its people? What kind of government ignores the needs of its population while prioritising its own interests? Instead of increasing spending on essential services such as education, health, social services, and legal support, these governments repeatedly cut funding to all of them. At the same time, they continuously increase their own spending, allowances, and incomes, while claiming to serve the people—when in reality, they are only victimising them.

Under the Western government system, many people go without their basic living necessities, including food and medication, to the point of starvation. Numerous disadvantaged families with large numbers of children struggle daily to feed them, let alone clothe or medicate them. Many of these families are forced to listen to the cries of their children, who beg for a new pair of shoes, a new shirt, or even essential medication that their parents cannot afford.

Yes, these are facts—occurring right here in so-called civilised Western countries.

Are the elected governments of these "civilised" Western democracies aware of these realities? How could they not be? So what have these governments done to address poverty, starvation, and the lack of medical care for children living under their authority and within their borders? They turn a blind eye. They let the starving starve, the sick die, and those suffering from untreated pain lose their teeth, their health, and eventually their lives. Such people are deemed unworthy—denied education, denied hospitalisation, dismissed as expendable.

Under the Western system, many families cannot even afford to give their children a proper funeral when they die. Some children are considered “fortunate” to die young rather than grow up immersed in this culture of wolves.

How does someone who is widely unpopular become the Prime Minister of Australia? Is there even one honest politician among them who is willing to stand before the people and speak the truth?

His unpopularity is a well-known and widely acknowledged fact, discussed openly across communities. Since he became Prime Minister, scarcely anyone has spoken positively about him. No one openly claimed to have voted for him, anticipated his rise to office, or believed that he should hold such a position.

The overwhelming belief was that he was incompetent and unfit for the role—that he neither had, nor ever would have, the interests of Australia or its people at heart. Many consider him the worst Prime Minister this country has ever had, deserving a place in the rubbish heap of history. The question remains: how did he become Prime Minister if hardly anyone voted for him? When people speak of his time in office, they speak only of disappointment, disbelief, and suffering.

How did he remain in power for two terms despite his ever-increasing unpopularity? Once again, the last thing anyone could have imagined was that he would win another term. Yet all he had to do was follow the instructions of those who placed him in power, and he could remain there for as long as they wished.

Even if it meant walking over the dead bodies of the weak and innocent, destroying families, shattering the hopes of young people seeking education and employment, and forcing countless individuals to live in constant fear of whether they would have enough money for their next meal. If they survived all of that, then the government-supported drug industry stood ready to finish the job—ensuring that people either lay down and die or became so powerless that they could no longer challenge the criminal system whose true objective is the destruction of the masses.

What kind of logic is this? A government that deals in drugs and sells them to addicts. What is this nonsense about the "Swedish Model" or the "Swiss Model"? Such claims are repeated only by those who refuse to confront reality. Who are these so-called exemplary societies? What are their crime rates, divorce rates, numbers of unlawful and unwanted children, levels of drug use, alcohol addiction, and suicide?

What kinds of sicknesses and social diseases do these corrupted societies suffer from—and inflict upon themselves? Over the years, have they improved their social conditions? What has happened to family ties? What kind of relationship now exists between parents and their children?

Children who were once taught to bow, respect, and kiss their parents' hands now take their parents to court, sue them, and attempt to have them imprisoned. Children seek to lock their parents away. How does a mother feel when she must stand in a witness box and be accused of neglecting a piece of her own soul?

This is the mother who endured abuse from her own children—the son who slapped her face, the daughter who kicked her stomach. The mother who never ate until her children were full, who never slept while one of them coughed at night, and who rose at dawn to ensure her child was still alive and well. This kind, compassionate mother is beaten, accused, institutionalised, or even stabbed to death by the very children who believe she belongs in prison or a mental institution.

What happened when parents once disciplined their children? What kind of societies existed then? How much love and compassion did children have for their parents? What achievements did they reach through education? What kind of lives did they lead? How many ended up in prison? How many had unlawful children? How many died from drug overdoses?

Why has the situation been reversed, so that children now discipline their parents? Who is responsible for this reversal? Who benefits from it? Are children truly better off now, or are both parents and children suffering and being destroyed? How many parents accept or agree with this system? How many have the freedom to object? And more importantly, who would listen to them if they dared to speak out?

Why must parents lose their children—who in most cases are their only assets, and in many instances the sole reason they live? Who is taking children away from their parents, and for what purpose?

Is this truly a sign of civilisation? Can such societies be held up as models or examples? Are they progressing forward, or sliding downhill toward destruction?

Have these societies retained any family values at all? Are they happier societies than they were thirty or forty years ago? Are they better off in any way, shape, or form than they were decades ago? Have they genuinely improved themselves?

What has their so-called technology done for them? They have more spare time on their hands—so how is that time spent? Certainly not on raising their own children. Children are handed over to childcare centres to be raised by the government and its system. Nor is this time spent caring for elderly parents, who are instead placed in nursing homes, waiting to die.

What did these "civilised" societies achieve with their civilisation? What did they gain from their technological advancement? Buttons to press to do everything—and then what? Board a plane to cross oceans in a few hours, work fewer hours, and spend the extra time watching television, drinking alcohol, and using drugs.

These societies, often held up as models of civilisation, are nothing more than examples of destruction—examples of moral collapse, of the extinguishing of the human spirit, and of criminal governments exploiting their own sick, weak, and vulnerable populations. These are governments that will stop at nothing to gain total control, regardless of the cost.

How do people feel after consuming alcohol or drugs? Do they feel happier—internally or externally, physically or emotionally? Are they better off in any way at all? Why do they continue to do it? Do they know it is harmful? Is this self-harm, knowingly inflicted?

If ordinary people lack the logic or awareness to recognise what harms them, what about the government that claims to protect their lives, well-being, and interests? Why do governments allow people to destroy themselves? Or is it the

government itself that organises and masterminds the harm inflicted upon humanity?
What kind of enjoyment can anyone gain when their mind is absent due to alcohol or drug consumption? What price do they pay? In many cases, the cost is their own life. Such a person becomes incapable of living a normal life, pursuing education, or performing even the simplest work. They exist only to die, their entire life reduced to suffering.
Everything around them becomes ugly and painful. Many people choose to remain asleep, wishing never to wake again, unwilling to face another day in which their dreams turn to ashes, with no hope, no prospects, and no future.
What do they look like the next day after consuming drugs and alcohol, after sleeping in different beds night after night? Are most of these people truly happy, content, and satisfied with this kind of life, or do they merely pretend to be so because it never occurred to them that there is another way for human beings to live?
Those who control the lives of the people do not want them to know that an alternative exists. Those who control everyone and everything want drug and alcohol consumption to continue. They decide how much to give, how much education to allow, how much unemployment to create, and how much treatment to provide. They want people to remain under the influence, because once addicted, people devote their entire lives to obtaining substances.
No time remains for them to think about who is in control, who governs their lives, or who truly runs the show. Those performing on the stage do not realise that they will eventually die for the entertainment of

those watching from the seats. And once they die, they will never wake again to receive applause. A new show, with new actors replacing those who died, begins immediately.
Is this life nothing more than an act? Do people have any choice in the roles they play, or must they accept whatever role is assigned and continue until the end? Have they ever considered another way to live? Has any alternative ever been presented to them?
Do people truly believe life is a joke—that they arrive whenever they wish and leave whenever they choose? Do they live according to their own desires, or according to the wishes of those who control them when they have lost control over themselves?
Which human being can claim to have chosen to come into this world? Which can claim to decide when to leave it? Even if someone dies in the street from a drug overdose, he still dies only when his time is complete. Even suicide succeeds only when one's appointed time has arrived. Many have attempted to take their own lives and failed, living many years afterward. The time of departure is never a personal decision.
Is this life truly uncontrolled, governed by no authority at all? Those who believe they control everything are ignorant of the fact that they have no control even over their own existence. Can any of them choose to live one year, one day, or even one second longer once their time has come?
Can anyone claim that they were meant to die yesterday or last year, but decided to remain alive longer? If they believe they control everyone else's lives, why can they not control their own? Why can they not live forever?

No—they are not in control of anyone or anything, not even their own destiny.

Human beings have no control or choice over when they enter this life or when they leave it. However, they do have full and unconditional choice over how they live while they exist on this earth. Some choose to place themselves under the control of others, to live beneath their feet, and to devote their lives to the pleasure of those who dominate them—often without realising that they were not created to serve other human beings.

Others choose to spend their lives under the influence of drugs and alcohol. Yet every human being has been given intellect; no one was deprived of it. That intellect can be used to think deeply and seriously about the reality of existence, and when used sincerely, it leads to conclusions that make complete sense.

Every minute, approximately one hundred people die across the world. That is six thousand every hour, nearly 150,000 every day, and close to forty million every year. This has been happening for thousands of years. Where do all these people go after they die? Is there another world?

If one believes there is no world beyond this one, and that death is the absolute end, then life becomes meaningless, purposeless, and uncontrolled. This leads us again to the fundamental question: why are we here in the first place? It was not our choice to arrive in this world, and it will not be our choice to leave it. Yet while we are here, it is our choice how we live.

Every human being will one day leave this world—this is undeniable. Even those who believe in nothing cannot deny death. Death is the only certainty guaranteed to every human being. The rich will die, and the poor will die. The beautiful will die, and the ugly will die. The sick will die, and the healthy will die. The old will die, and the young will die. Men will die, and women will die. The unemployed will die, and so will Prime Ministers, Presidents, Kings, Queens, and princes. Everyone will die—sooner or later. If not today, then tomorrow.

This is the one fact that deserves our full attention. We should not concern ourselves with when death will occur, because when it does, nothing can prevent it. What we must concern ourselves with is how it will occur. In what state will I be when it happens? What beliefs will I hold then? What will I carry with me? Am I prepared for that moment, which will come without doubt, sooner or later?

Will it be too late to prepare then? How many people have returned after death to prepare themselves? None. So what makes anyone believe they will be different? Preparation must happen now, not later.

Have you ever seen anyone take their possessions with them after death? Have you seen anyone buried with their wealth, gold, or treasured belongings? Have you seen anyone so attached to another person that they entered the grave alive to accompany them? We know this never happens.

Every day we see people, regardless of status or possessions, go into the ground alone and empty-handed. Yet this is where many people make a critical mistake: no one goes down alone.

If life were merely a joke—uncontrolled, purposeless, with people coming and going as they pleased—then existence would be meaningless. But we know this is not the case. So what, then, accompanies every human being when they die? It must be something that makes sense—something beyond food, drink, wealth, or possessions. We will no longer be able to eat, drink, spend money, bribe, buy, sell, or kill innocent human beings.

From the moment a human being is born, a record of deeds is created. Two angels—one on the right and one on the left—are appointed to accompany that person throughout their life. Every action, no matter how small or how great, is recorded. When death arrives and the person is placed in the grave, that record is closed and sent down with them. That record is the story of their life.

You were free to act as you wished during your time on earth. Now that you have left this world, you have entered another—one in which no further actions are possible. A world where you can no longer kill innocent people, drop bombs on children, starve populations, or prevent medicine from reaching the sick. No more lies, deception, cheating, or betrayal. No more committing adultery against a spouse who trusted you. The time for action has ended; the time for accountability has begun.

This is your own account, and you are your own witness. No excuses, no denials. It is your own record, and you will not be able to reject it. Who will help you then? Who will defend you? Who will carry any portion of your blame?

You thought you were created in vain, left free without consequence, on a journey with a beginning but no end. Now the journey has ended, and you face the result of the test you were sent to undertake. How much injustice did you commit—against others and against yourself?

Did you believe your body belonged to you? It never did. It belongs to its true Owner—the One who formed it while you were still in your mother's womb. You assumed you had the right to abuse this body with drugs and alcohol. Who gave you permission to do so? This was injustice against your own self, and injustice was never permitted—even against oneself.

Who permitted you to give away parts of this body—your kidney, your heart, or other organs? Do you believe yourself more merciful than the One who created those with illness or disability? Do you think the Creator was incapable of creating them without defects, just as He created you? Do you imagine their condition was a mistake?

You claim kindness after death by donating what never belonged to you. But how kind were you while alive? How much harm, oppression, and injustice did you inflict upon others? Now you wish to appear virtuous by offering parts of a body filled with hatred and denial of its Creator.

This error only deepens when those who accept such parts seek to prolong their lives at any cost. They too were dissatisfied with how they were created and failed to recognise that their condition was a test. Those who perform such operations will also face death, and on that day, they will no longer be able to claim noble intentions. Their true motives will be exposed.

They hoped to create life by transferring parts from one body to another. Let them create even a single fly, if they can. This is the challenge that has stood unanswered.

Those arrogant human beings who failed to recognise their Creator will one day meet Him and be held to account. Let them do as they please while they are able—they are free to choose. But the Day will come without doubt.

The last day will come—there is no doubt about that. It is the Day of Reckoning, the Day of Account, the Day of Justice. On that day, every human being ever created will be gathered, with their record hanging from their neck. It is a day of terror and truth. No injustice will be done on that day, and no soul will be wronged.

Those who believed, who followed the commands, rules, and guidance of their Creator, will not be harmed. Those who did not wrong themselves or others, who recognised and worshipped their Creator as He ought to be worshipped, will succeed.

Human beings should reflect deeply on that day, whose arrival is beyond doubt. They should live their lives in a way that makes them successful and victorious when that day comes. They should prepare themselves for their meeting with their Creator and change their way of living to align with His commands.

There is an alternative to drugs, alcohol, and the destructive paths that governments of darkness promote—paths that encourage humanity to harm itself and others. This life will end sooner or later, and once death arrives, the Day of Reckoning begins for each individual. How many millions of human beings have already faced their reckoning? Yours will come as well—sooner or later.

Are you prepared for it? Whether you are ready or not, it will not miss you. It is fixed. It will reach you wherever you are.
Save yourself from eternal punishment. This is not a matter of ten, a hundred, or a thousand years—it is forever. What risk are you taking if the questioning in the grave is real? This is a serious matter, deserving serious thought.
Examine, study, read, research, and use your intellect. It will guide you. It is not difficult to recognise that this world was created, and that human beings were placed upon it for a purpose: to recognise their Creator and to be tested in how they live.
Good is clear, and so is evil. The Creator has commanded human beings to do good and to refrain from evil. This is the essence of the test. If we obey, we succeed; if we disobey, we bear the consequences. We are accountable only for our own actions. We are not responsible for the wrongdoing of others, so long as we advise them, encourage good, and prevent evil whenever possible.
Following the commands of the Creator can only lead to happiness in this world and in the Hereafter. This truth has been deliberately concealed from the people by the criminal governments of darkness, whose only concern is their own interests. They exploit the people to fulfil their material desires in this rapidly ending world.
These governments misrepresent facts, hide the truth, and prevent many from practising their faith. They make every possible effort to misguide the masses and divert their attention away from recognising their Creator.

Recognising the Creator and worshipping Him accordingly is the true purpose of human existence. This is the reason human beings were sent into this life. To fail in this task is to defeat the very purpose of existence.

For example, horses were created for people to ride. If you were to see someone carrying a horse instead of riding it, you would immediately recognise that something is seriously wrong. That person would not be using the horse for the purpose for which it was created. In fact, you would consider such behaviour irrational, because it reverses the natural order and places unnecessary hardship on the individual while providing no benefit.

Using anything for a purpose other than what it was created for always leads to difficulty and loss.

This world, and everything within it, was created for the benefit of human beings and to serve them. We are meant to use this life and its resources to reach our final destination—the Hereafter. If, instead, we place the world on our heads and serve it, rather than allowing it to serve us, then we have failed our purpose.

Human beings were created to worship their Creator—this is the true purpose of life. Those who forget their Creator and devote themselves entirely to material pursuits, wealth accumulation, and worldly achievements are misguided. They chase luxury, power, technological achievements, and grand constructions, while neglecting the reason they were created.

In doing so, they waste their short and valuable time on matters that offer no real benefit beyond this life—things that will inevitably be left behind.

Many of us, in our pursuit of wealth and fame in this world, have lied, cheated, deceived, stolen, bribed, and committed many other sins. These are our deeds. These are what we will take with us—not submarines, jumbo planes, or high-rise buildings.

Just as we would consider a person who carries a horse instead of riding it to be irrational, those who truly understand the reality of this life would also see the obsession with material gain—at the expense of the Hereafter—as equally irrational. To devote one's entire life to accumulating worldly possessions that offer no benefit in the everlasting world is a grave mistake.

What would happen to Western governments if people stopped drinking alcohol, smoking cigarettes, and using drugs? Not only would these governments face bankruptcy, but they would also be confronted with healthy, clear-minded individuals—people with the intellect, education, and awareness to challenge corruption and injustice.

Such people would expose government schemes and manipulations. They would reveal hidden intentions, demand accountability, and remove corrupt officials from positions of power, placing them where they belong.

This is precisely why criminal governments do not want people to become intelligent, aware, or capable of questioning authority. This is why governments permit—and even encourage—the drug trade. Drugs do not enter a country without government approval or assistance. Without permission, such substances could be stopped easily if there were genuine will to do so.

Many people wonder what these governments truly plan and what they hope to achieve. Whatever their objectives may be, they are never aligned with the welfare or interests of the masses. Their sole aim is total control over everyone and everything.

The system of Islam stands ready to be implemented once the governments of darkness—along with their criminal, corrupt, evil, deceptive, discriminatory, victimising, racist, and hypocritical systems—collapse.

(10)

Globalization
The New World Order

The idea of globalisation is to place everyone, everywhere on the surface of the earth—every human being, every government, and every political, social, financial, economic, educational, commercial, medical, pharmaceutical, cynical, and radical system in the world—under the control of one global power.

That power would have total, ultimate, and complete control over all these entities: complete control of every government in the world, and accordingly, complete control of the masses through their corrupted governments, appointed by this ultimate global power. This global power would make every decision that affects the world—from which government should come to power next in any country, to what people should have for breakfast in that country.

This global power would have the entire world under its control and could lead it in any direction it wished. It would be capable of making the whole world adopt one policy and one philosophy.

Those who are critical of this process argue that such concentration of power risks undermining national sovereignty, democratic accountability, and cultural independence. They believe that global institutions and influential actors increasingly shape policies that

affect governments and populations worldwide, often without direct public consent.
From this perspective, global power structures influence which governments rise and fall, what policies are adopted, and how societies are directed. The concern is not that one authority literally controls every detail of daily life, but that decision-making is increasingly centralised, leaving ordinary people with diminishing influence over matters that affect them.

Critics argue that globalisation promotes uniform systems

- education systems shaped by shared international standards,
- justice systems influenced by external legal frameworks,
- economic systems governed by trade rules and financial pressures, and
- social norms guided by global media and cultural industries.

Such uniformity, they argue, reduces diversity and limits the ability of societies to define their own values and priorities.
One education system would be imposed in which children are not to be disciplined by teachers or parents. Decisions would be made about who can become a lawyer, who can become a doctor, and who should not be educated at all.
One justice system would exist in which criminals are protected and allowed to go free if they have connections with, or have worked for, the global power.
One economic system would allow countries to trade only in certain goods, import or export only specific

products, and do so with selected countries only—resulting in the global power deciding what people can eat and what they can wear.
One social system would dictate how people live their lives and spend their time: what social activities are acceptable, what sports to play, what music to listen to, which pop groups may visit which countries, what clubs may be established, what television programs may be watched, and what movies may be shown.
One political system would exist in which a global government appoints every government in every country. It would decide how many parts a country should be divided into and which countries should be removed from the map altogether.
The global government would decide what to do with the world: what religion should be practised, which human race should be wiped from the surface of the earth, what currency all countries should use, and what language all people should speak.
This global government would have the power to move masses into the middle of the ocean and abandon them there, or lift masses into the sky and fire missiles at them. It would possess the means, the power, the wealth, the technology, the intelligence, the resources, the governments, the armies, the helicopters, the tanks, the submarines, the satellites—and most importantly, the most powerful tool of all: control of the global media.
They would rely heavily on the media to convince the masses of their objectives and to justify their actions in destroying lives, killing civilians, and creating wars against the weak, the unarmed, and innocent women and children.

In what direction do they intend to steer the world? What are the real objectives of this global government? Will there be freedom? Will there be justice or individual rights? Will there be any right to negotiate, object, or refuse?

Globalisation, as presented here, is a dictatorship—far more evil and destructive than any system the world has ever known. Its grip is so strong that it becomes a matter of do or die. The global government would not hesitate to destroy anyone or anything that stands in its way or attempts to expose its intentions. It is their system or nothing.

Their stand-alone, globalised system would be identical in every country. Through it, they would achieve their goals with hardly anyone able to challenge them.

The global government would be the only authority permitted to rule any country. At present, almost all governments—except for a few small regions—represent this global power.

Their first move was to bring every government under their control. They decide, choose, and appoint their next man or woman in every part of the world: Australia, Indonesia, the USA, the UK, and almost every Muslim country. With the exception of Sudan and Afghanistan, they continue to work toward installing governments there as well.

The global government uses its most powerful tool—the media—to install its chosen governments. Then comes what they present as democracy: elections. These are used to convince the masses that they chose their leaders, even though the decision was made long before any vote took place.

Governments that no one voted for, approved of, or could have imagined would come to power are made popular by a corrupted, one-eyed, hypocritical media and installed accordingly.
A major concern raised by critics is the role of global media. Media outlets, often owned or influenced by powerful corporate interests, are seen as shaping public opinion, framing political narratives, and legitimising policies that serve global economic or political agendas. In this view, media becomes less about informing the public and more about directing perception.
This leads to a fundamental question:

Who benefits from globalisation, and who bears its costs?

Will individuals retain meaningful freedom?

Will justice remain impartial?

Will dissent and alternative viewpoints be respected?
In larger countries such as the UK and the USA, this process is less obvious. Preparation begins years in advance, but the outcome remains predetermined.
As seen in one of the most scandalous elections in the USA, the global government's chosen man came to power despite serious credibility issues. In normal circumstances, such a person might be denied even basic employment, yet he was entrusted with leading a nation—though he made no real decisions himself. Such individuals are easier to control. Their records can be used against them whenever they show resistance. When Clinton hesitated to follow orders,

pressure was applied through scandal. He learned quickly and complied.

To its critics, globalisation resembles a form of soft authoritarianism—not through overt force, but through economic dependency, cultural pressure, and institutional control. Opposition to this system is often marginalised, dismissed, or portrayed as irrational or extremist.

Many believe that modern political systems increasingly offer the appearance of choice rather than genuine participation. Elections may occur, but policy directions often remain unchanged regardless of which party or leader is in power. This fuels public disillusionment and mistrust.

On a global scale, critics argue that military alliances, defence spending, and foreign policy decisions are often driven by strategic and economic interests rather than the genuine security needs of populations. Smaller nations may feel pressured to align with the priorities of more powerful allies, even at significant economic or social cost.

In countries like Australia, public attention often focuses on domestic issues, while foreign policy and defence arrangements receive less scrutiny. Critics argue that this leaves important decisions largely unquestioned.

From a religious and moral standpoint, some argue that globalisation conflicts with divine guidance and ethical principles. In particular, Muslims who hold this view believe that Islam offers a complete moral, social, and legal framework intended to guide humanity toward justice, responsibility, and accountability.

They argue that Western secular culture—characterised, in their view, by materialism, moral relativism, and social fragmentation—has failed to provide lasting solutions to humanity's problems. Issues such as inequality, social breakdown, exploitation, and conflict are seen as evidence of systemic failure.

Supporters of this critique point to the growing number of individuals worldwide who are seeking meaning, structure, and justice through faith, including Islam. They see this as a response to dissatisfaction with prevailing global systems.

From an Islamic perspective, this moment represents a call to responsibility—not domination, but justice; not coercion, but moral leadership. Islam, they believe, offers principles capable of restoring balance, dignity, and accountability.

Despite the immense power of modern institutions, technology, and military force, believers hold that no system can prevail against divine truth. They see history as evidence that material power rises and falls, while moral principles endure.

The global government miscalculated only one thing: the strength of Islam. No matter how powerful they believe themselves to be, they cannot change what God has decreed. Islam is the final system for mankind.

Western culture, adopted by this global power, has collapsed and has nothing left to offer humanity. Its corruption, injustice, and moral decay are increasingly visible—even to Westerners themselves.

Despite all efforts to suppress it, Islam continues to grow. The global government has failed to realise that the world is indeed being prepared for one system—but not theirs.

Parents and teachers understand the importance of discipline, yet the global government seeks to abolish it. Children are encouraged to rebel, while authority is transferred from families to the state.

As families weaken, children grow dependent on the government, not their parents. Family bonds are destroyed, replaced by loyalty to the state.

Social systems are engineered to undermine families, promote dependency, and replace parental authority with governmental control. Parents become caretakers of children who increasingly belong to the system.

The absence of discipline leads to social collapse. Youth are lost to drugs, exploitation, and neglect, while institutions profit.

This world is like a ship: if a hole is allowed, everyone sinks. The responsibility placed upon Muslims is to prevent that collapse by restoring justice, order, and morality.

Despite all power and weaponry, the global government cannot overcome Islam. Its influence continues to grow, even in places where it is most opposed.

Australia, like many countries, is affected through internal manipulation, economic pressure, military dependency, and foreign influence. Defence spending, fear campaigns, and forced alliances serve the interests of others, not its people.

The USA's military-industrial system relies on global conflict. Allies are drawn into its agenda, regardless of the consequences.

Yet despite all this, the system they oppose continues to rise.

From an Islamic perspective, the answer is clear. Justice does not originate in power, but in truth. Authority does not belong to those who possess force, wealth, or influence, but to those who are bound by moral responsibility. Islam is presented here not as a cultural identity, but as a comprehensive ethical framework—one that challenges any system that places human ambition above divine guidance.

Islam cannot be defeated. Its growth is unstoppable, its foundation firm, and its future inevitable.

The future of the world will not be decided solely by technology, wealth, or force, but by the values that guide human action. In that struggle, ideas, beliefs, and moral conviction remain as powerful as any system ever created.

(11)

GOVERNMENTS, LEAVE THE KIDS ALONE
The Fallen Generation

As a Muslim family living in the West, we had to fight against all the odds to preserve, protect, and defend our faith in Islam. Western governments, Authorities, and organisations automatically assume that even if you came from an Islamic background, once you are in the West, you have to do what Westerners do. An eyebrow will be raised at you if you look like a Muslim, act like one, or dare to make any Muslim demands, from the schools where your children are attending. Like asking for your children to be excluded from Christian preaching classes. Or, that certain parts of their bodies, not to be exposed, during sports activities, or not to go away on school camps for one week, where teachers consume alcohol and perform sexual acts, in front of the students, and encourage the students to do the same.
Taking advantage of the students, being at a difficult and critical teenage period, in which it is hard to control their desires, and the students being away from the supervision and the guidance of their Muslim parents. Muslim parents were automatically branded as fanatics once they asked the teachers to exclude their children from the Christmas celebration. The teachers and the school would then intensify their efforts towards those children, whose parents want to

bring them up as Muslims, to take these children in the opposite direction of the Islamic teachings. A Muslim woman who wears a scarf, not minding or caring, or making any requests, or giving teachers any instructions, regarding her Muslim children's religious requirements, is treated differently by the school and its staff. Such a Muslim woman would be welcomed, smiled at, and spoken to by all teachers and staff.

She would receive encouragement and support for herself and her children. Her children would quite often be rewarded when they were not deserving to be rewarded. These are all signs by the school to show their approval of the trend, of such a family to adopt a Western lifestyle, and to encourage them to adopt and introduce more Western habits into their life. On the other hand, the Muslim mother who gives instructions and makes demands regarding her children's Islamic requirements is often treated with disrespect, often ignored by teachers and staff, and no one wants to speak to her. Her children are always criticised, always branded as underachievers, never awarded, trouble makers, and a decision is made that they will never have any chance in education or employment, even if they were extremely clever and intelligent.

At a very early age, children and their families are sorted out, and efforts are made to change the attitude and the way of thinking of those Islamists, to win them over, and basically, Westernise, or more precisely, Christianise them. These types of families are closely monitored by the authorities, a record is made for them, all their movements are watched, and continuously documented.

Strange enough, living in a Muslim country until the age of twenty, I was never a practising Muslim. Having come to the West, to start a new life, to realise my dreams, and to do what the Westerns do. Soon, I was confronted with the true face of the West, and found myself asking, is this what you really came here for? Is this what you really want from life? Is this what the West is all about? After a long and hard struggle, I found my way back to reality, to the truth, to the real inner peace, just like someone who dropped a precious diamond in the mud, then picked it up, cleaned it, and started to look at it, as if he were seeing it for the first time. Then, started to admire and appreciate its beauty and magnificence. Oh, how did I ever forget that I have Islam inside my heart? It was the mud, the filth the dirt, the lies, the deceiving, and the injustice of the Westerns, that made me see, the truth, and the longer you live in the West, the more you become aware, that it is the culture of wolves, that violates, and strips mankind, from all their rights, making every effort to keep humanity in the darkness, away from the truth, and the light and the guidance of Islam. Many Muslims, unfortunately, are unable to see and realise how precious the diamond they have, because it is covered with mud manufactured by the West.

My real confrontations with the West's injustice and hypocrisy began when my children were about to start their first year at school.

When the children entered schools to start their first year of schooling, we explained to teachers and principals that we are of the Islamic faith, and there are certain things that we do not do, and certain activities that we do not take part in; issues of that

nature should be considered when dealing with our children.
We made the school aware that our children do not eat any kind of food. Music, dancing, drawing of Christmas trees, and swimming in the Western traditional swimming costumes are all sensitive issues. Older children have to observe fasting during the month of Ramadan, and there is no camping or excursions where the students will spend a night away from home. No sex education, no drug education. Then came the most important request that made all authorities declare war on us, it was the demand that our Muslim girls be allowed to cover their heads, and the school uniforms be slightly modified to suit Islamic instructions.
The war went on, and is still going on, and it will continue till we die. They have all geared up against us, schools, hospitals, government organisations, the justice system and the police.
We have been confronted with the real picture of the offending West, with its lies, deceptions, corruption, injustice, manipulation of opinions, misrepresentation of facts, and attempts to get Muslims to criticize, denounce and testify against Muslims.
From that point on, discrimination and victimisation started. How dear we ask to have a separate, unique identity, and make our own decision regarding what suits our children, and what does not?
This is a Western country with a Western culture, which totally contradicts all Islamic teachings. They did not agree or accept that our children should refrain from smoking, using drugs, drinking alcohol, going to discos, nightclubs, wild parties, or walking

naked in the streets. They did not have much hope in achieving that with the older generations of Muslims who were born overseas, but they held great expectation for the younger Muslims to be like them, follow their foot steps, turn against, and reject their own parent's Islamic identity, and for that they have declared war against us over our children to take them away from us. They have plotted, planned, changed, and modified their systems to get Muslims children away from the religion of their parents. They would break any rules, do away with any law, pay any price, to prevent the creation of a young generation of Australian true Muslims, and if such a generation must be created, it has to be a Muslim generation, Western Style.

A generation that if such a war broke out between Australia and Indonesia or Malaysia let a lone the Middle East countries, this new Muslim generation would be among the Australian soldiers who would not hesitate to drop bombs on the heads of their own grandparents, uncles, aunties, or any other relatives who may live in the same home where their own parents may have once lived.

All schools, particularly the ones with a high percentage of Muslims students, had special plans for those students. Muslim students are encouraged to take part in non-Islamic activities. The schools stated to students that their parents need not know what they were doing at school, and they have no right to question them about anything.

Quite often, parents' permission is not required or totally ignored, implying parents' insignificance in deciding their children's school activities.

Police officers were brought to visit schools regularly, telling children about their right to speak to their parents, and the police phone number was given to children as young as five years old. The message was that the police are there to protect you from your enemy, that is, your parents. This was more than enough to corrupt the little minds of these children and get them to ask themselves, who are our parents? Later, in the first year of high school, the schools are visited by officers from the DOSS, telling the twelve-year-old children how much social security payment they will get if they leave home. Examining the changes that took place in the Social Security Act would not leave any doubts that all modifications are designed to encourage children to move away from their parents, especially Muslim parents. To become independent, do their own thing, be free, enjoy life, live it up. Until such time, when parents would be called to pick up the bodies of their dead children from one of the streets, or one of the hospitals, or one of the drug centres owned by the government.

The students are owned, and belong to the school or rather the Education Department, or more precisely to the Government, and parents have no say in the matter of deciding the type of activities their children take part in at schools.

The Arabic language was once taught only by Muslim teachers, who incorporated some Islamic teachings as well. To eliminate any religious teachings in government schools, all Arabic teachers employed in government schools are non-Muslims.

The school realised that many parents would not agree to many of the activities that the school asks the students to take part in, so to get around this problem, the school never asks parents' permission. Parents are often not informed about many of the activities that take place at the school.

Parents' religious beliefs are disrespected and considered inferior, and their children should be brought up according to the beliefs of the society in which the children were born. Children are taught to disobey, disrespect and rebel against their parents through the school counsellor, or programs specially designed for Muslim students that contain everything contrary to the teachings of the Islamic religion. These are all matters of reality that I have first-hand experience with.

Teachers are always absent or missing from classes, never replaced by other teachers. Classes are joined, thus creating a difficult learning environment affecting all students. Subjects other than what the students were supposed to learn are taught, which is often a brainwashing subject.

Many schools are left without principals for many months, with an acting principal who would usually have a teaching job, as well as being inexperienced and unable to run the school.

Sport activities are often exchanged, or replaced with other activities such as Discos, or going to the movies, without the knowledge or permission from the parents. Practising Muslim students who refuse to take part in such activities are usually put in detention so that next time they will learn to put the school activities above their religious beliefs. Others are encouraged to take part without the knowledge, consent or approval of their parents.

When sports activities were to be replaced, the program chosen to replace them is always offensive

to the Islamic faith. There would be no time to inform the parents or get their permission.
Excursion, Movies, Discos, and more, all behind parents' backs, which leaves no doubt that students attending Government schools are not worthy of receiving any education. Most of them are children of migrants, and therefore they should work as cleaners, rubbish collectors, security guards, which is another expression for police pets, or be unemployed and rely on the social insecurity system, of which the first lesson they received when they entered high school explained to them how to leave their parents and receive government support. Rent assistance if you leave your parents? Away from home allowance? Not happy with the way your parents treat you? Find out how you can get a new foster family with all expenses paid by the government? The new foster family will never question you about what time you come home at night. Or what kind of drugs should not be used? Or who slept in your bed last night? Or tell you that you should have an abortion, and should not keep the child, because it will ruin your future.
I recently Learned a new organization has been established by the government to assist young Muslims who left Islam, are thinking about leaving Islam, or need assistance to leave Islam. For the government to be innocent of any wrongdoing, the head of the organisation should be a Muslim scholar capable of justifying what cannot be justified.
This offending Western system is guilty of the crime of widening the gap between parents and their children, alienating children from their parents, and creating a shield where children cannot see their parents to look up to them, and parents cannot see

their children to give them guidance and advice. It is another face of a stolen generation, but in a much more cruel way. When something is stolen, it gets taken away from you; you do not see it anymore, and you may forget about it after a while, but when it is right in front of your own eyes, and every time you try to reach out for it, it falls and gets further away from you, it is a fallen generation. Parents have to watch with their own eyes their own children slipping away from them, day by day, drowning, and sometimes dying, and cannot do much to save them. In the few times when the parents were able to stretch their arms out to reach for their children, and the children responded, and tried to grab on to the hands of their parents, the system would not allow that to happen, and they were quicker to get to the children first, and stood between the children and their parents, preventing parents to provide any help or support to their loved ones.

Children aged 15 and 16 years old were shooting themselves inside the drug centres that the offending Western government opened for them, while their grieving parents waited outside, prevented from getting to them. They are the children of the system, owned by the system, and controlled by the system.

Why do seven- and eight-year-old children need to learn about performing sex and using drugs? This defies any logic that alleges to care about the welfare and the best interests of children. It cannot be disputed that such polices by Western governments could only be aiming to cause damage and create a new generation of kids who are addicted to destructive habits that would ensure they are doomed. Introducing sex and drug education at primary schools is a crime. Children who have been exposed to such learning from a very young age will not grow up to be normal, and their chance of survival as a decent human being is minimise, reduced if not eliminated.

Those Muslim children who refused to be part of this system, and continued to act like their parents, most of them are behind bars, given doses of drugs by force, by the prison authorities themselves, to make sure that these children will never again become well enough to think about Islam.

This is the government's new policy for the fallen generation. Who is responsible for this crime? How long do they think they will go on with such a plan?

This is their plan, but the creator of all mankind, Muslims and non-Muslims, has a different plan. See if you can stop it, see if you can modify or change it with all the technology available to you, and all the resources under your control.

Taking Muslim children away from their parents is not the kind of crime that any Muslim parent would accept a “sorry “ for it, from a Prime Minister of a racist country.

Stealing children away from their families is in itself a crime, but the biggest crime is what happens to those children when they are under the control of the government. Those children are often abused by the government organisations and their systems, which are often full of wrongdoers.

The government's recent drug policy is aimed at making the government the sole trader of all kinds of drugs. Our innocent children are taking away behind bars and given drug shots every single day to destroy their lives in a slow, and cruel way after denying them any chance of education, or employment, and demolishing their hopes for any future of any kind, and when they die, their bodies are cut to pieces, and sold as body parts, which is the crime that every single Muslim living in this country will have to answer for, when they stand before their creator one day. It is totally forbidden by the Islamic faith, and considered a horrific crime to touch the body of a dead person. Even after our children die, you still don't leave them alone, even when their eyes are removed. This is the Western Culture, the culture of wolves.

An appointed government minister would have a specific dirty task to complete. Once it is finished, by that time he would have started to smell badly, then he would be removed, after the government that he represents distanced itself from any responsibilities towards the dirty work that was carried out, and disapproved of what that minister did. Then he or she will go, and another minister comes with a new dirty task to accomplish, and would continue with it, again, until he or she starts to smell, he or she will go, and another will come, and so on. As soon as such a new minister comes, he or she would declare to the people, things such as that closing schools is not on his agenda!

By changing a minister of education, or a minister of police, or a minister of health, the government is fully aware that the people did not approve; in fact, they were angry about the closing down of schools, police stations, and hospitals. The government believes it could swallow such anger and improve its image by replacing such ministers, particularly if an election is near.

This is just some preparations that have to be made, but how the people feel, or how angry they may be, have nothing to do with a government remaining in office. The problem is more serious and much deeper than the replacement of a minister.
It is understood that Parliament is the place where elected members are supposed to govern. The term "GOVERN" in Islam means to look after, to serve, to provide and give, to attend to the needs of, to make sure no one is left without food or shelter, and most importantly, to provide protection from crime and criminals. In the Western system, those who govern are the real criminals. They are the ones who steal, deceive, cheat, corrupt, lie, rape, deal in drugs, and ask innocent young little boys and girls who sell their bodies in the street to survive to pay GST.
This is the kind of criminal and corrupt Western system that the government decided to adopt against the will and wishes of the vast majority of the people, Muslim or non-Muslim.
They keep on creating and introducing one new system after another to eradicate Islam, and the Muslims, including buying and paying some hypocritical people who claim to be Muslims, and put them in charge of the affairs of the Muslims, so that things would go according to the government's plan.
People are crying out for justice, which will never be achieved unless and until Islam returns to rule the world. And it is on its way. We as Muslims declare that we say NO to your corrupted social system of drugs, prostitution, and gambling.
All changes taking place aim at one thing, "more control", why? Because of fear, believing that more

control will provide more protection, and give the government the upper hand, but it will not.
The Western Culture now live in total darkness, unable to find its way, all attempts to put out the light of Islam have not succeeded, and it will never succeed, the light of Islam is increasing by the hour, and soon will destroy the darkness spread all over the land by the offending West.
They don't need any discrimination; they don't need more control
Governments, leave the kids alone
All they are is just another kid going to fall.

(12)

ISLAM AS A FORCE
The future is for Islam

The chaos that the whole world is experiencing today has come about because, for many years, Islam has been studied, thoroughly investigated, and fully understood by non-Muslims more than it has been studied, investigated, and understood by the Muslims themselves.

The non-Muslims have not been studying Islam as a religion, a faith, a belief, but as a force, an amazing force that once swept the world in such an incredibly short time like no other force, known to humankind ever did

That ideology of the force of Islam that concord the world, was comprehensive and complete. A unique, fully cooperative system that left nothing out and nothing uncovered. A system that did not, ever, need any changes, any modifications, any deletions or any additions. A system that has stood firm, untouched, unaffected and unchallenged, and will continue to stand as such till the end of time.

A complete system of all aspects of life. To fulfil all that mankind needs in this world. to be their economic system, political system, financial system, social system, educational system, commercial system,

medical system, health system, and above all, their spiritual system.
More importantly, to teach, to educate, to inform, to enlighten, to show, to prove, to warn, and to explain about the hereafter to all mankind. To promise the hereafter. To tell about the other world that we have been created for. Soon or later, we have to leave this temporary world to go there. To the everlasting world, in which we will remain for eternity. Provided that we understood the teaching, the education, the information, the showing, the proof, the warning, the promise, and were enlightened by the light of Islam.
Long ago, the non-Muslims fully understood that if the Muslims were left to practice and apply the faith of Islam in their lives, this world would remain under the control of the Muslims alone. For as long as they were practising and applying this force in their lives.
If Muslims were to apply the force of Islam in their lives and their societies, and Islam were to continue to be practised correctly by Muslims, not only would the whole world be under the control of Islam and the Muslims, but also no other force would have been able to exist, let alone be in charge of world affairs.
Over the years, the disbelievers have miserably failed to fully suppress and control the power of Islam, let alone preventing the Muslims from practising it. The disbelievers over the years have changed their plans, their plots, their ideologies, techniques, policies, approaches, and their methodologies in their struggle against Islam.
They have refined their war ideology. Confrontation has always given the opposite results, and it is no longer the way to deal with an unbeatable force. The methodology of sanctions, no trade, no

industrialisation, no manufacturing, no import from the Muslims, no export to the Muslims, no education, no water, hunger and starvation for Muslims, all of these approaches, did not enable the disbelievers to have any control over the Muslims, and Islam continued to spread, and to be practised more than before those sanctions were applied.
If Muslims are practising and applying their religion to their lives, then they will be in control of this world. If Muslims are in control of this world, then they must be practising their religion. No way Muslims would be in control while not practising. No way Muslims will be practising and not in control.

Islam is a force that has to be applied, untested, untried, and unchallenged. No other force ever existed, or will ever exist, that would have the same uniqueness, the same ideology, the same completion, the same strength, the same affirmation, the same offerings to its followers, who have unprecedented devotion to this force.
Islam is a force, unique, unimaginable, everlasting, with endless, miraculous power that would not negotiate with, tolerate, or accept any other power to stand next to it
All other known powers have disappeared forever. With the remaining Western power on its way to disappearance. The whole world is watching such meaningless power shrinking by the hour, sinking in the darkness of its unimaginable sins, while the whole world is watching the light of Islam, appearing once again to replace such criminal, injustice, corrupted, evil, foolish, oppressing, misguided, satanic, ungrateful, sinful, shameful, and wicked power.

The world's present powers are standing powerless in the face of the return of the old warrior that accept no injustice of any kind, no wrongdoing of any kind, and no oppression to any of mankind, Muslims or otherwise.

They do not have the intelligence, the intellect, the knowledge, the understanding, the ambitions, the readiness, the willingness, to join such a power as the power of Islam, rather than, standing on its way, and against it, rejecting, objecting, opposing, denying, lying, preventing, resenting, deceiving, and disbelieving that the power of Islam has come back.

The disbelievers fully realised that, with all their powers, they may only be able to delay the return of the power that no one can stop from coming back. Thinking, the delay was according to their plan or resulted from their powers, and controls, while the delay was, and is, because those who will receive, and be in control of such power, were not, and are not ready yet, and not prepared as yet, to be in charge, and take control. More calamities, disasters, suffering, and sacrifice are still required to refine those who will be in control. So, the coming back of that force, the force of Islam, would not be a hasty return.

The powerless superpowers, doing everything they can do, or even things that they cannot do, or are not capable of achieving, to delay the return of the force of Islam, and change its direction from heading towards the West.

They used unimaginable power to prevent the force of Islam from appearing again in Europe, Yugoslavia and Albania, but they are standing hopelessly against the appearance of the force of Islam in France,

Germany, the USA and the UK. They are changing their laws every single day to deal with the spread of the force of Islam. To give it no chance of having any power on the lands of the West, the evil West, the offending West, whose power has to wind up soon making room for the unchallenged power, the unique system that will deal with all the problems, sickness and diseases of the world. The system will be welcomed by many Westerners, along with many Muslims. Westerns who have long suffered, been humiliated, and mistreated under their own uncivilised Western culture, that has long used, and abused women and children, in an attempt to change their real identity, and their real biological forms, and turn them to other sort of creations whom they were never created to be, and get them to perform sinful acts, and shameful jobs, for the pleasures, and the benefit of the sick power that is in control of their lives. The power of Islam will be welcomed by Western victims who had never seen justice and had been waiting for the alternative that would replace the injustice they had faced all their lives. This world will never see real justice until Islam returns.

In their attempts to delay the return of Islam, they have snared many Muslims under their wings, trying to convince them that the West is there to stay, to win, to dominate, to control, to decide, to give and to take, to kill and give lives. There have been many losers who have adopted and followed the West in every aspect of their lives. One question we have for those is, where will the West end up? Well, you can go with the West, where the West is going. You can sink where the West is going to sink. You can burn where the West is going to be burning. Do not change your

minds when you see the real fate of that culture, which you once thought was so great, and you would do anything to be one of them. To be a Western, to dress like them, eat like them, drink what they drink, smoke what they smoke, dance as they dance, sing as they sing, and marry as they marry.
It is only fair that those who adopted the lifestyle of the West should go down with the West when it goes down soon.
The West does not want or wish to go down alone; they want to take as many Muslims as they can, to go down with them.
They have used all their means and ways to attract Muslims to their Western culture and Western way of life; they attempted to Westernise whole countries, including the replacement of the language of that country by English or French to replace the language of the Koran.
The West fully understands, fully realises, fully aware, fully confident and sure that the force of Islam is about to appear soon.
All the West's attempts to prevent, or even just to delay that force to return, have miserably failed, and the face of the force of Islam has started to look over the entire earth once more.
The West has now given in and accepted that the force of Islam is here, and it is here to stay. The West, breathing its last breaths, is trying to plan and plot how to survive in the presence of the force of Islam.
The West's latest and newest method in dealing with the force of Islam is to try to negotiate a solution for the power of the West to survive or remain along with the power of Islam.

The West has lately come up with the idea of " Uniting all religions". In such a criminal approach to dealing with the force of Islam. The West started to spread the idea that all religions are the same, came from the same source, and call for the same basic beliefs. They even went to the point of admitting that Jesus was a human being, which is the major conflict, but not the only one, between Islam and Christianity. Thus, narrowing and closing the gap between Islam and all the other religions that exist in the world today. If the West succeeds in achieving that, then the religion of Islam would accept and recognise that other religions that exist in today's modern world have rights to exist, to be practised, and accordingly must have a form of power to represent them, which is the West. The West is seeking permission from the forces of Islam to exist by presenting itself as the representative of the Christian faith.

Under the "United Religions", the West hopes that there will be no enmity between Islam and all other religions. Islam will no longer consider the other religions to be wrong, incorrect, inaccurate, changed over the years, and have been corrupted; therefore, it will give all other religions legal rights to exist. Under such a plan, followers of other religions are no longer considered as disbelievers, and therefore, no longer considered as opposers to the Islamic faith; accordingly, they are no longer the enemy of Islam.

The West, having failed in all its attempts to prevent the force of Islam from returning, is now saying, we are all the same, no difference between us, our beliefs are the same as yours, and yours are the same as ours, let us be united under one religion, and worship in God. This is exactly what the disbelievers had said to the Prophet Muhammad, peace be upon him, when they saw that the force of Islam could not be stopped or challenged. They said, " Let us worship your God one day, and you worship our God one day. The answer to that proposal came from God himself in a verse of the Koran that many Muslims recite in their prayers every single day, including today. This is Sura Al-Kafereen " The Disbelievers". Oh Muhammad, tell them, Oh you Disbelievers, I do not worship what you worship, and you do not worship what I worship, you have your religions, and I have mine.

Any Muslim who accepts the idea of one religion is one of the disbelievers. When the force of Islam comes to put the world back in order, before starting to deal with the real disbelievers, it will deal first with those so-called Muslims, who sold their religion for a low price, and for a small gain, who are followers of the disbelievers, and whose ideology serves the evil intentions of the offending West.

The West, over the years, has, and continues till this very moment to kill innocent Muslims by the thousand every single day, children being slaughtered, women being raped, and Muslims all over the world are subjected to all imaginable, and unimaginable torture, and punishment simply because they are the worriers of Islam, and because they refused to be the tails of the offending West.

The West, which is terrified of the return of the force of Islam, is now saying, " Let us forget the past, and be united under one religion. The West with its untold crimes that wiped out entire human races, the West that invented the Aid Virus to wipe out, of the entire surface of the earth, millions of innocent people in the

African nations, the West, the number one enemy of Islam.
Islam is a force that stood alone, and once more soon it will return to stand alone, without any compromising, any negotiations of any kind, without any concessions of any kind to anyone, or by anyone, a system that will be applied, untested, untried and unchallenged.
The God of Muhammad has never given his prophet peace be upon him any rights to negotiate or to compromise on his behalf.
Any Muslim who may call himself Muslim, attempting to negotiate, or give any concessions or compromise on behalf of our Lord or his prophet, should be given the news now that his place in the lowest level of the fire of hell is guaranteed.
The idea of one religion is the newest invention of the disbelievers and their hypocritical so-called Muslim associates, who will join the disbelievers and stand behind them on the day of reckoning
The group of God, the followers of his prophet, are to establish God's commands on earth. To rule and be in control, with their feet made firm, not affected by the disbelievers, and the misguided, applying God's laws alone. No other solutions, no other alternative. They will never accept the desires, the hopes, the wishes, and the false beliefs of the hypocrites and the disbelievers. No other beliefs, no other ideology, no other law will be deemed to exist along with the force of Islam.
The West, which has, over the years, changed its planning, its plotting, its techniques, its policies, its approach, its ideology, its method, and its warfare,

has now to bow down, accept defeat, move aside, for the force of Islam to bring justice to the land.

(13)

THE POWER OF ISLAM
The Sorting Out

The world will soon have to turn to the only system that will save mankind from all the tribulations they have been experiencing for many centuries, under the Western criminal system. It will have to turn to Islam and reject all other ideologies.
The West is living in fear. The fear of the return of its number one enemy, Islam.
Islam is a real threat to the very existence of the West. If Islam were to return to rule the world, it would mean, by all counts and all probabilities, the very end of Western civilisation.
Even the mere fact that, applying a small part of Islamic rules, at any stage, will mean, and result in, the West losing its power, its control, its domination, its influence, its effect, its respect, its wealth, its rules, and its culture would be buried under the ground, with its corrupted, materialistic, uncivilised, unjust, inhuman, destructive, and criminal system.

The application of one single rule of the Islamic Shariah (law) is more than sufficient to put the Western culture and its system to shame. If for example, the chopping of the hands of the thieves, and similar other approach, to other kinds of crimes is adopted by the West, this will guarantee, to eliminate crimes, and there will be no need, for the failure prison system, which did nothing, but providing, a training ground for criminals, to learn and become experts, in the new methodology of crime techniques, then, they were graduated, to commit more sophisticated kind of crime, encouraged, and motivated, by the West's corrupted, and criminal justice system.

The more they try to paint Islam with the colour of blood, the more people turn to Islam. Every single day all over the world, thousands of people from all walks of life, of different nationalities, different colours, different races, different intellects, different levels of intelligence, different ways of thinking, different backgrounds, and different education, become Muslims.

One day, I asked an Englishman who newly embraced Islam what made him turn to this religion. His answer was a unique one, which I never come across before. He said, because of the bad publicity! I asked him to explain what he meant by that. He then told me, for many years, he watched the world media, presenting Islam as a fanatic faith, with rules suitable to the stone age, uncivilised, in some instances, out of date, and cannot be applied in this sophisticated time and age. The Muslims were always presented as savage, bloodthirsty terrorists. He thought to himself, Islam is supposed to be a religion from God, as Muslims claim; such a religion cannot be all that bad, if the word God is clinging to it? After doing a lot of research and studies on Islam, he, one day, said, I want to be a Muslim. He is now not only a Muslim, but a devoted one; he allocated a lot of his time to tell everyone about his trip, from a vaguely believing Christine to a devoted Muslim.

The stories of the countless numbers of those who turned to Islam have always put me to shame, as someone who was born a Muslim. The devotion of those who newly turn to Islam has always struck me. The pronunciation and memorisation of a book of such size, as the holy Koran, without one mistake, of one word, or one letter, by people of non-Arabic-speaking backgrounds, cannot go along with any logic. Children, again, of non-Arab background, some as young as six and seven years old, had memories of the whole of the Koran and reciting the whole book, without making one mistake. If an Arab tries to speak to these children in Arabic, he will find that they do not understand one word of Arabic. Yet, they were able to read the whole book of the Koran, which is written in Arabic, memorise it by heart and recite the whole book without a single mistake.

I have always found that to be the most astonishing living miracle, apart from the miracle of the construction of the Koran itself, and the miracle of its contents. Who can remember two or three pages of any book of any kind, in his own native language, and recite them without making a mistake? Let alone doing that in a language which you do not know or understand?

The Koran is 114 (surah) chapters, with some 600 pages. There are a lot of similarities between some of the sentences and chapters, making it even more difficult not to mix one sentence from one chapter, and allocate it to a chapter that it does not belong in. Yet those whom Allah (swt) has gifted and chosen to

memorise his book, their recitation is, with 100% accuracy. Despite their young age and the fact that they do not speak Arabic.
The systems, in all the different Western countries, are almost identical. The education system, the social system, the justice system, the health system, the economic system, and the political system, one system fits all. All, on the defensive side against the unique system of Islam. Money is their game, and remaining in control is their greatest concern. They are all united under one goal, one ideology, one aim, one thought, one objective, one purpose, and one benefit, that is, to eliminate Islam. Or, at least, reduce at any cost, the power of the only system that poses real threats to the foundation of their existing Western system.

They are terrified, paranoid of not being able to protect their system and ideology, on their own soil. They want to extend their defence, outside their own territory, to secure and ensure that the threat, the power, and influence of Islam do not reach their lands. That was their plan, not realising that Islam has been implanted, on their own soil, so deeply rooted that it can never be removed.
The West, fearing the power of Islam, extending to and affecting its system, tried to extend its Western system to be applied, and to influence many Muslim countries, by preventing these countries from applying any Islamic rules. To the West's way of thinking, one single country applying Islamic rules is dangerous enough, and if Islamic rules were established in one country alone, it would be more than capable of overthrowing all Western

governments in no time. Therefore, the West is willing to sacrifice anything to ensure that not one single Muslim country has a truly Islamic government. When a Muslim country comes anywhere near having an Islamic government, all Western countries will declare a state of emergency, often, even a war would be declared, to prevent that from happening. All the Western countries will get together, forget about all their differences, and the trade problems they have among themselves, and they become united, and they are all out to kill that Islamic government before it is even born.
They will use any tricks, any methodology, any technique, any power, any force, any destruction, even if they have to kill every single human being at that spot that poses a threat of establishing an Islamic government, they will do it, without any hesitation. If they feel that the people of that country are really after an Islamic system, and it was hard for the West to eliminate that country, then, they would have no choice but to appoint their own Islamic government, which is, in no doubt, an Islamic government Western Style. An Islamic government that receives its revelations, guidance and instructions not from God, but from the West. Just like what happened in Indonesia and Somalia.

Why is the West terrified of Islam? The UN was created solely for that purpose, to ensure that no Islamic government ever makes its way to power, anywhere in the world. This has always required long-term planning, a huge amount of resources, and highly trained personnel specialised in Islamic affairs. It required complete control over every Muslim country, through the control over the government that rules that country. Such governments, even though they have been appointed by the West, would now and again allow some Islamic activities to take place, some Islamic groups or Islamic movements to be present. On one hand, to present themselves as Muslims to their own people, on the other hand, to play games with the West. These kinds of games are mainly to manipulate the West, to accept some of these governments' demands, which would mainly be a request to remain in power for another term, a matter that may not be according to the West's agenda. As the West may, for many reasons, have planned a change of government in that country. These governments, by allowing some Islamic activities to take place in their country, will enable them to negotiate deals with the West, in return for keeping that Islamic movement under control.

If the West refused to bow to that government's demands or did not provide assurance to that government that it would return to office after the coming election, the result may be an Islamic uprising or an Islamic movement coming one step closer towards forming a government in that country.

Sometimes, the West itself allow some Islamic movements to be present in some countries, for many, known or unknown reasons.

The West would have to do its calculations very fast and decide to give in to the demand of that government, or to try to establish and organise another government to be put in power, with new promises made by the West, to that government. Sometimes the West attempts to negotiate with that new Islamic movement in that country, which wants to come to power and rule that country. The West will attempt to do that, only if they can see a very high rate of success, of turning that new Islamic movement into an Islamic movement Western style, in return for helping that new movement to come to power. The West would always succeed in such deals, as many of those so-called Islamic movements are not truly Islamic and in many situations, such movements were, really, after gaining power, and they used Islam only to get access to rule the country. Therefore, such a deal with the West comprises helping them to gain power, in return for some Islamic concessions from the new Islamic government, and perhaps, a few Islamic FATWAS, that will ensure that such a government would be, in front of the West, when it is time, to be admitted to the fire of Hell.

It came to the West's attention that some Muslims, in Yugoslavia, started to practice Islam again, after all the efforts made by the West's long-term planning to eliminate Islam from that region of the world. A state of war was declared by the West to investigate what went wrong, and why the West, which thought they have buried Islam in Yugoslavia, had failed, and how some signs of Islam could still be present in that country?

The West's investigations found that, in Bosnia, one day the Muslims woke up to find the Serbs turning their guns at them. The Muslims asked, why? We have been living together for many years, we eat what you eat, we drink what you drink, we dress like you, we lay on the beaches naked like you do, our only religious celebrations, is your Christmas, your boys marry our girls, we are exactly like you we,

speak the same language, so why are you turning your guns at us now? Then came the answer, yes, it is true that you are very much like us, but you still have Muslim's names!
The West's investigations discovered that the West had made a fundamental mistake when they allowed the Muslims people in Yugoslavia to continue to carry Muslim names, which remained, to constantly remind them that they are Muslims. Despite all the effort made by the West to remove any ties that a European country like Yugoslavia may have with Islam, there were still some signs of the presence of Islam remaining there.

The West's approach to dealing with the appearance of the shadows of Islam in Yugoslavia was totally regrettable from many Western political observers' point of view, who believed the outcome had exactly the opposite effects. The West decided that the way to deal with this problem was to hit hard at the Muslims in Yugoslavia, whose only connection to Islam was their names.
The crimes committed in Yugoslavia, by all the offending Western notions, can never be told, nor can they be imagined; it is unprecedented in the history of mankind. It was all aimed at getting the Muslims there to change their minds about Islam. It was an issue of belief, a test for Islam. Many of the orphan children, who witnessed the slaughtering of their fathers and the rape of their mothers, were taken to the merciful West, to be brought up as Christians. The issue was purely a religious one.
The West once more was, in a real and direct confrontation, with Islam. To learn that Islam can

never be fought. The West had every imaginable tool at its disposal; they had the power, the technology, the computers, the personnel, the equipment, the bombs, the jets, the tanks, the communications, the spying facilities, and most importantly, they had the Serbs. The Bosnians, on the other hand, had nothing whatsoever. Not even food or drink. Yet, the West did not win the war in Bosnia. The result of the war in Bosnia was that Islam has returned, in a very strong way, not only in Bosnia, but in the whole region, where Muslims, who totally forgotten, that they were once Muslims, started to check their names again, to discover once more who they are, and what they are capable of achieving.
The West, by hitting hard at Bosnia, had greatly contributed, towards the return of Islam, and had helped many Muslims, to wake up, and discover themselves as Muslims, once again, and realise their real mission in this world, and they are not here, in this world to follow, anyone but, for every one else to follow the Muslims. What the Muslims in Bosnia realised after witnessing the massive killing that took place there was that we are not here in this temporary world to stay, and we go to the hereafter sooner than we think.

The price the Muslims had to pay, in Bosnia and Kosovo, was very high. But the lesson that the Muslims learnt from Bosnia and Kosovo was that, if the Muslims totally forget who they are, their creator will even get the disbelievers to come and remind the Muslims that they are Muslims, and cannot be anything else. The creator, once more, demonstrated to us that his promise to his prophet, to look after this

religion till the last day of this world, will always be kept, and this religion will remain, for as long as this earth remains in existence.
The West's experiment in Bosnia and Kosovo was a major setback for the West, which became aware and learnt that Islam is on its way back to rule the world. The West has also learnt that, using force against the Muslims, even though they may only be Muslim by name, would most certainly result in a stiff resistance from them, leading to a speed-up of the return of Islam. That is why the West is now using a totally different approach, in Indonesia, trying to eliminate the use of force from both sides at any cost. The West, once again, mistakenly thought that an agreement with the Indonesian government was an agreement with the Muslims of Indonesia.
All the West can hope to achieve in Indonesia is to delay the Islamic extension into the West in general, and into Australia in particular. Yet the Australian governments, over the years, except the Keating government, had failed to recognise that Islam can never be prevented from entering this country, and attempted to eradicate Islam and the Muslim people, living in this country, in such a non-political, illogical, and unintelligent approach.
Those governments have continuously accused the Muslims of organising crimes, falsely accusing the Muslims, by the corrupted media of Australia, on almost a daily basis. Leading to bad publicity against Muslims living here, all have proved to be unfounded. Their efforts resulted in many Muslims returning to Islam, and their statistics will prove that as a result of this continuous hatred, and animist Islam is on the increase.

The Keating government is one government that, to some extent, took the real interests of this country at heart, and realised the importance of having a real and true relationship with Indonesia, and accepting Indonesia as a Muslim country, without trying to Christianise the largest Muslim country in the World. The Keating approach to Indonesia was not accepted by the USA, which really cares about its own interests alone, and the interests of Australia mean absolutely nothing to it. The USA sacked the Keating government in the following election, even though almost everyone voted for the Keating government. Paul Keating knew that the reason he lost a winnable election was that a comment he made when he was visiting the USA, when he told the American government to mind its own business, and not to interfere in Australia's foreigner polices. That was enough for him to lose the election, despite his popularity and despite the unpopularity of his opponent. At that election, the people of Australia could not imagine that they could put up with having to see his opponent's face, presented by the media, as the PM, every day.

The Howard government did exactly as told by the USA, which is why they even won another term, when it was easily said that he is the worst PM this country ever had.

Australia has fully adopted the polices of the US. After having the reputation of being a peaceful, multicultural country, it is now one of the most racist countries in the world. Following in the footsteps, and under instruction from the USA, it has declared itself as an enemy of Islam and the Muslims people.

Muslims living in this country have now started to experience a great deal of discrimination and racism, like never before. This has included assaults on Muslim women, stepping on the holy book of the Muslims, the Koran, and kicking older Muslim men while they were performing their prayers. The USA is now satisfied that Australia has recognised itself as a Western country, which cannot be anything but an enemy of Islam. We are yet to see the results of this radical change in Australia's foreign policy, which was only made to satisfy the USA.

The power of Islam will be demonstrated in every part of the world, including Australia. It will not be stopped, it will not be prevented, and it will not be delayed. The result of failing to recognise Islam as a power was the first step towards the downfall of Western civilisation. The West has made the fatal mistake of trying to suppress the power of Islam by force. Or by trying to negotiate with some Hypocrite Muslims, who, in no way, represent Islam or the opinions of the vast majority of Muslims. The West, till today, is not fully aware of what the Muslims really want. Trying to gain some ideas from the hypocritical Muslims, who only misled the West for some materialist gains, for themselves, and who do not care about Islam, nor do they care about the West..

The West does not know what Islam is all about. Who are the Muslims? More importantly, what are the Muslims capable of, with the will of Allah? Therefore, the West is not prepared and not capable of standing against the power of Islam. The West, instead of inviting destruction upon itself, could have taken a totally different approach, which may have given it the chance to continue to exist under the umbrella of Islam.

The West, by declaring itself the enemy of Islam, has resulted in Islam being the enemy of the West.

To minimise the amount of suffering, the power of Islam should be recognised by the West and should be met with the appropriate understanding and acceptance, not by illogical rejection and denial. The real suffering here is the suffering of the Westerners, who die every single day without being really exposed to the true Islam. Without being offered the chance to realise that there exists another faith, another religion, that came from God after Christianity, that is worth considering, and worth thinking about, before they can just reject without knowing anything about Islam.

This is the biggest crime they can commit against themselves, to die without allowing themselves to examine Islam. The enemy of Islam cannot give them a true picture of Islam.

In that sense, true Muslims consider that a country like Afghanistan is one of the luckiest spots on earth. We, as Muslims, can see that every single day, hundreds of people from Afghanistan get admitted to paradise, before the first drop of their blood reaches the ground. Who seems to have all the power? And who seems to have nothing? Yet, who is living in fear, and who is calm, content and happy to die? You be the Judge.

It is not known, and we as Muslims cannot predict, if this round of confrontation between Islam and the West will be the one that will bring Islam back. When that will happen is all in the hands of Allah (swt); He will decide.

True Muslims, however, would wish that it would not happen that soon, as the vast majority of Muslims are not ready to receive Islam after being under the influence of Western culture for so long. If Islam were to come back now, many of those Muslims will be treated as Westerns, as they look like, act like, and live like Westerns. There has to be a period given to the Muslims to sort themselves out, and make up their minds, where do they belong, that is to consider (You either with us, or against us).

This is the period that we are going through now. It will be up to Allah (swt), to decide when the sorting out is to end. Then, the victory and the punishment will come together. Sorting the believers from the disbelievers, and the Hypocrites.

As Allah (swt) will establish his religion on earth, with the power of Islam, through the true believers. From this perspective, we see that the Afghans who die every day are the lucky among us Muslims, because they already know where they stand and where their final destination is. We do not know where we will be when the sorting out starts. More precisely, where will we be when the sorting is finished? We, as Muslims, should strive so that our place would be, with the power of Islam.

(14)

TO THE MUSLIMS
You Are The Superiors

Muslims should be strong; their strength should be generated from being believers. They should never be weakened or grieved. As they are the superiors. They should have the upper hand and been the highest among all other nations if they were true believers.

Muslims have been created, produced, and brought forward to all mankind to be the teachers, the preachers, the leaders. To be in charge, responsible, watchful, and the guide for the human race.

To lead humanity from darkness to the light, to prevent people from doing evil and to order them to do good. To stop people from worshipping the creations and get them to worship the creator, to divert the attention and the concentration on this temporary, narrow, and limited world, to the wide, unlimited, and everlasting world of the hereafter.

Muslims have been created to fully practise the religion of Islam, demonstrate the greatness of God, and apply God's rules and laws on earth, and ensure no other law or rules are to be practised or carried out along with the law of Islam. Muslims are ordered to struggle until such conditions are achieved.

Muslims are ordered to fulfil their duties, as have been ordained by God, towards their own individual selves, towards their immediate family members, towards their communities, and towards all human beings.

Muslims are ordered to represent Islam, and invite all humans to recognise their creator, who created everyone, and everything, the one and only, one creator who has no partner, no father, and no son. To him we belong, and to him we will return, and we will be questioned. Muslims are ordered to give a reminder, as a reminder is beneficial for the believers. What preparation have we, as Muslims, made for the hereafter? Are we going to leave this life one day and go somewhere else? Where will we be going? What is waiting for us there? No one, not even a disbeliever, would deny that one day, he will have to leave this world. So leaving this world is an unquestionable issue. It will happen soon or later. So, are we ready for that time when we have to leave? Will we get any warnings? First call, second call, or it will happen all of a sudden in a matter of seconds, without any warning. Will we have time to get ready and prepare ourselves, maybe pack our bags? What happens if we are not ready? Could our departure be delayed? Could we ask for an extension of time? Or, could we ask for another chance? Was anyone ever able to delay his departure from this world? Or, when it is time to go, it is time to go?
If it is your time to leave now, are you ready to go? Will anyone ever be ready? Who is? This process consists of one second; you are here alive, the next moment you are there. You are in a different world, for which you should have prepared yourself. What preparation have we made for that moment? The

moment that comes without any warning, without any signs, or any forewarning. What have we got ready to take with us? We may have around us our wives, our children, our parents, our close family and dear friends, but which of them can we take with us? And even if we could, would the most beloved one to us and by us be prepared to go with us when it is time for us to go? What other things that belong to us could we take? Our university degree, our business, our bank books? Did any of those who went before us take any of these things with them?

We spent our whole life to obtain this degree, to obtain that house, that car, and to save that much, but would any of that be of any benefit when it is time to leave? We know, we have to leave it all behind. Where is the logic here, when we spent our entire lives collecting what would be of no benefit to us, when we go from this world?

What mistake could be more horrific than someone making the wrong preparation? What kind of loss is it going to be when we take the wrong road right to the end, only to find out that it was the wrong road? We have the knowledge that once we get to the end, we can never turn back and start again. We have the undeniable knowledge that there is no second chance. So, as we go along, shouldn't we again and again check to see where we are going? Ask ourselves, is this the right way? Are we heading in the right direction? Are we following the right path? Many, once they become aware, they are heading in the wrong direction, they stop, and then start to look and search for the right way. They open their eyes and see many signs and many indications

that tell them something is wrong. That can never be the right way. Where am I heading? What is going to become of all that? Once someone starts to search for the truth, he most certainly will be guided, quite often before he reaches the end of the road.
Others are content with whatever they are doing and wherever they are heading. They are not willing to think, re-examine, or do some research to find out if they were heading in the right direction or not. They are satisfied with their situation in this world. They continue that way, to find out, only when they reached the end, that what they earned, acquired, possessed, and obtained were all useless and of no value.
Then, some know and know that they are heading in the wrong direction. Yet, they insist on going that way. They defy everyone and everything, without realising that they are only defying and harming themselves.
Many do not fully realise that we are engaged in a very serious business. It is the business of no second chances. This life is not a joke. The biggest joke that someone can play on himself is to think that he is free to do what he likes, and that is it. Many like to do wrong, and like to continue to do wrong, but for how long?

Taking the wrong road to the end, only to find out and realise that we made the wrong preparation, is the worst thing we could ever do. That is to say, that acquiring the house, the car, the degree and the bank account were the worst preparations we made. Worse still, if we do not even have the house or the car and have nothing in the bank, yet we made no other preparation as well.

What preparation do we need to make, and how soon do we need to make it?
We claim we want to go to paradise, but what preparation have we made for that? If we were going to move from one place to another, we would start to make preparations. Packing up and moving furniture and so on. If we were going to go on a trip overseas, we would buy the travel tickets, get the necessary visas, and so on. If we set our mind up to get higher education or further training or obtain certain qualifications or a degree in some specialised field, we start to prepare for the exams and the tests that we have to sit for, to get that degree or qualifications, sometimes years beforehand. What preparation have we made to get to paradise? Do we want to get there without being prepared, and without being tested, and without doing the necessary training that qualifies us to get there? For everything else in this life that we want to acquire, we need to make efforts to obtain it; we have to go through many tests and exams to prove that we qualify to acquire such a thing. Yet, we want to get to paradise without making any efforts for that, and without being tested, to see if we qualify and deserve to get there. We believe it is an automatic process, free for anyone and everyone. Would that be justice? What kind of preparation is required from us to get to paradise?
It is not building high-rise buildings, jumbo jets, and submarines. It is not acquiring wealth, nor is it the striving for power and fame. None of this is needed. How to get there is clearly described in the Koran and in the teachings of the Prophet Muhammad. If we look for guidance in any other sources, we will never be guided, and we will never get there.

We can value ourselves. We know exactly, and better than anyone else, what we are doing, what our real intention is, and what is inside our hearts. Is it this life or the hereafter? We should ask ourselves right now, what are we thinking of? Is it this life or is it Islam and our faith? What does my plan for tomorrow include? Making effort for this life or for the hereafter? Then ask yourself whether you are ready to get to paradise? or you still have a lot of things you want to finish off here? Even at the last moment of your life, you will still not be ready when the angel of death is in front of your own eyes. You will ask for an extension. Not even to offer two raku salah (short prayer) will you be given that. It is time to leave with the condition you are in now, and with the preparation that you have made, whatever it is. You are not going to say SHAHADA (witness that God is one and Muhammad is his messenger, as your last words), except and unless you have lived for it, and according to its rules and commands. A Muslim who defied and disobeyed the orders of God, and did everything to destroy the Sunnah (teachings of his prophet), is he going to say SHAHADA as his last words? Only God knows best.

Be informed that you have a DOUBLE that remains with you, from the moment you were born. It never leaves you; if you look after your double and are kind and generous to it, it will look after you. If you neglect it and insult it, it will neglect you and insult you; this double will be buried with you. This double is your deed.

What preparation have we made for the hereafter, the everlasting, eternal life?

We collect what we do not need, and neglect what we do need. This is the big loss, we soon find out that. If we spent our lives looking after our good deeds, then, when we go down in our graves, we would find that we did not need these good deeds, which would not be so drastic. But, if we do not look after our deeds, and we go there to find out that we do need them, what will we do then? We cannot have another chance; no one ever did. This will be the biggest loss. A punishment forever and ever will be waiting for us. We are the losers, the fuel of the fire, who have been prepared for those who will return to their creator with the wrong belief. For the Muslims, no wrong belief could be worse than believing that what you need to take with you is a fancy car, a beautiful house, or silver and gold. A good Muslim must know what he or she needs to take with them, and to start the preparation now. Do you not know how much time you have left? This is a temporary life, a deception and an illusion. It is not the real thing; we will soon go from here. The most important thing that should concern us is how we will go? Under what condition? What will our last words be? Are they going to be my house, my car, my business, my money, my job, my degree, my family, or are they going to be my creator, my faith, my prophet? This is what will determine what will become of us after our departure. Our last words will only be according to what we have spent our lives on. If my life were spent on getting the house, then my last words would be the house, the house, the house, and so on. If I never knew who my creator is, how can his name be among my last words? If I did not know what my religion is all about, never prayed, never fasted, never wore Hegab or covered myself the way a Muslim woman should cover, then how can Islam be among my last words? If I did not know who my prophet is, who the example that I should follow in my life, my actions were totally against his teachings, how can the prophet be among my last words? How would the angels recognise me, in my grave, when they come to question me, and they found that I have shaved my beard and grown my moustache? What proofs would I have then, that I am a follower of that prophet? The angles will not check your ID or your death certificate to see if it has a Muslim name, but will check your book. The book that contains every little thing that you have done all your life. The book that was kept by the two angels who accompanied you all your life.

An angle on your right and another on your left were appointed to record everything you did, good or bad. That book will be closed by those two angles and will be sent down with you when your trip here ends, and your trip into the other world begins. The angles of the grave will receive you with your book. You will not be asked your name, or who you are, or where did you come from, or what is your title, or what is your position, makes no difference whether you were a king, queen, a president, a prime minister, how old, how young, how rich, how poor, what was your qualifications, how much money you had, how many children, how many wives. You will never be asked any of these questions. There will be three questions, which are all you will be asked, and they all have to do with your belief. We knew all about these three questions while we lived in this world. Not only were

we given the questions that we will be asked in the grave, but we were also told how to answer them. Yet many of us will fail. Because at that time, only what is in your heart will come out. What you lived for and spent your life with is what will be your answer. Oh, what a loss! This is a time when no one can lie, only the truth and nothing but the truth.
Building big houses, acquiring more wealth, more children, higher education, and further training, is that what we are doing? Is that going to get us to pass the test?
Ask yourself, what are you going to return to your creator with? Do not take anything that he did not ask you to bring, do not go to him with sins and shames, with disobedience to your parents, your husband, or a desertion of your brothers and sisters, and the rest of the family. Go back to him with the belief that he is the only one. To be able to justify that to him, you have to live your life according to his rules. This will get you to know him, and tell him when you meet him that you know him.
The materialistic means of this world are very important and very dear to us. Because we invested in them, we spent our lives, our times, our blood and sweat to acquire them. We could not tolerate anyone taking them away from us, or even attempting to cause any damage or defects to those things that we believe that we earned and own.

We would go crazy if someone scratched our new car. If a child threw a rock that broke a window of our new house. We would not be able to sleep for days if we felt that someone was after our jobs. We would not tolerate it if we did not have as many customers entering our shop on a day. We would think of killing our children if they did not do well on their exams. We may commit a crime for the sake of any of these important and dear things to us. We understand the value of all of these things because we have sacrificed our lives to acquire them. Its value is deep in our hearts. We want to look at these items and think about these issues all the time, and admire and praise ourselves for what we achieved. It is natural that when you sacrifice to obtain anything, the value of that thing must come into your heart. We generally adore this temporary world because we have sacrificed our lives for it, and we want to stay here forever if the choice were ours, so we can acquire more, be more proud of ourselves, and our achievements.

What happens when someone tries to scratch our beliefs? Or throw a stone at our faith? Or, did they attempt to tear our religion apart? How many effects would that have on us? How much are we moved when little Muslim children are slaughtered, and young Muslim girls are raped and tortured? Those who still have Muslims heart inside them, and still consider themselves to be Muslims, upon seeing what is happening to their Muslim brothers and sisters all over the world, the most they could do is to say to themselves

" Oh, how cruel", but the vast majority are totally cut off from the UMMAH (the nation of believers). The UMMAH should be like one body; if a part of that body is injured, the rest of the body must feel the pain. The UMMAH that forget who they are, what they are and why they are here in this world. Why they were

created, and what their creator requested from them to do. Most importantly, what is their duty towards the rest of mankind, who are not part of the UMMAH? This UMMAH, that became content, and satisfied with this deceiving, ugly world, and started to live for it, only for it. This UMMAH, that instead of being the leader, became a follower of the misguided and the cursed. This UMMAH, that fell into the traps of Satan, and surrendered its heads and its hearts to its gladiator. This UMMAH, that has given up on the promise of their creator, and felt that the road is too long, and too hard, and accepted this world as their final goal and their final destination. This UMMAH, that took their enemy, and the enemy of their creator, as a friend, and followed its footsteps in all directions, took the laws of their enemy as their constitutions. Doing away with the rules of the one who made them, and everything else. This UMMAH, which is supposed to lead all mankind out of the darkness into the light, they themselves walked right into the darkness, and became unable to save themselves, let alone anyone else.
The UMMAH that followed the instructions of their enemies, that led them to destruction, and left the guidance of their faith, that would earn them honours, respect, superiority, and make them prevail over everyone and everything.
The duty of this UMMAH is to lead all mankind from the darkness to the light, to strive for the world hereafter, and prepare for it. To act as a witness that those disbelievers did not obey, did not follow, did not practice, and defied the signs of their creator. So that, when those disbelievers receive the punishment they

deserve, the witness UMMAH will confirm that this is justice.

The whole world is in chaos since this UMMAH left its job, which this UMMAH has been sent to do. It neglected its duty, which it has been appointed to carry out.

What is the biggest crime that this UMMAH has committed, and is guilty of?

This UMMAH is guilty of failing to present Islam to the rest of the world. It has failed to challenge the different governments of the world, which prevented this UMMAH from doing its job, misleading the UMMAH, and deceiving it, into believing that the rule of the creator of all mankind is not suitable, or worthy of applying and practising in this time and age. These governments fully understood that these rules of Islam are the best solution for all the problems the world is facing today. The only reason these governments would not adopt these rules is that these rules are well known to be part of Islam, and they do not want to adopt Islam.

This UMMAH is guilty of not defying those governments and slipping through to their nations to present the truth to them. They have been waiting for the truth and for the message of Islam to be delivered to them correctly. People are dying every day without having the chance or the opportunity to get to know real Islam. It is the duty of this UMMAH to strive against any government that stops in the way of the truth being presented, and the light being held up in the middle of the darkness created by these governments and their evil system.

This UMMAH must have no doubts that it is holding onto the truth. The true faith, the true guide, the true and correct belief, which is the only salvation for all mankind, and the only faith that should be practised and followed on this earth.

Islam must be presented, at any cost. This is our real battle, which we must fight; this is our real goal, our real job, which we neglected for a long time. Everyone who considers himself to belong to this UMMAH must take it upon themselves to carry out their part of this mission. No matter what price we have to pay, and what kind of hardship we may face, Islam must conquer the world once more. Every Muslim is a solider, in the army of Islam, conveying the message of Islam is our real battle, and we must expect to face opposition, and hardship, but the most dangerous opposition is the hidden one, just like the one we face in this country, when they tell us, we have freedom to practice our faith, and in every possible way, they are putting obstacles in our way, to prevent us from practice our faith, let alone conveying it to others. They tell everyone that we are criminals, they let us build Mosques, and then tell everyone that those who attend the Mosques are drug dealers, and rapist, and the whole suburbs where Mosques are are the worst, and most dangerous areas, and no one is safe to walk there alone.

TO THEM, we say, the Dogs bark, the Caravan goes on, Islam is here to stay, Islam is here to dominate, to rule, to control, to prevail over and above all other religions and beliefs. IT is the only religion that God would accept from all mankind to follow, to practice,

and to leave this world and meet him with. The religion of God is Islam and nothing else.
The disbelievers have made a lot of efforts against us Muslims. Anyone who makes an effort, on anything, is bound to have some results, to the effort made.

24 hours a day, seven days a week, the disbelievers are making efforts to get the Muslims out of Islam. The disbeliever realised that getting Muslims to turn to another religion is something that will never happen. It is unachievable and unattainable. The disbelievers cannot even hope or think of that, but what they can hope for, and have succeeded in achieving, is to get Muslims to follow and copy them. To convince the Muslims that the way of the disbelievers in enjoying, living, utilising, benefiting, gaining and doing things in this world is better in many ways than the Islamic way.
The disbelievers plan to undermine the Islamic way of life and promote their corrupted, criminal, immoral, and destructive way of life. Which would lead them, and those who follow them, to the eternal punishment in the fire of Hell. The disbelievers are motivated, encouraged, and supported by their big leader, Satan, who plans and plots for the disbelievers on how to misguide the Muslims.
Many Muslims, as a result of the disbelievers' continuous, non-stop efforts, have been misled, tricked, deceived, cheated, trapped by the disbelievers, and have come to believe that, at least some of the ways of the disbelievers are good, worth following, adopting and did not see any harm in introducing such ways and habits into their Islamic homes. Many Muslims were not fully aware that the

introduction of such foreign habits into their Islamic way of life is destroying the very foundation of their faith.
The disbelievers are more than happy and more than satisfied just to see one Muslim adopting one of their ways or habits. To them, this is a real success, even if that Muslim who eats, drinks, and dresses like them still carries a Muslim name.

Just like we Muslims feel happy and content when we see a woman from among the disbelievers coming to Islam, covering herself and wearing Hijab. The disbelievers, no doubt, feel happy just to see any Muslim adopting their way of life. For the disbelievers, a Muslim adopting their way of life is a big win for their culture, their philosophy, and their way of thinking. It is viewed by them as a support for their system. On the contrary, when a disbeliever enters Islam, we Muslims do not see that as a support, or as a win for Islam, but rather, a win for the person who saved himself by entering into Islam. History stands to demonstrate that the religion of Islam is never affected by the number of its followers. Islam had the same strength when it was followed by one billion people as it had when it was followed by one man only. Islam is never honoured by anyone following it, but those who follow Islam are honoured by belonging to Islam.
Another huge and fundamental difference, here as well, is that, of course, when we invite them to our faith, we intend to lead them from the darkness into the light. To save them from a severe eternal punishment that is waiting for them. To direct their attention from this ending of the world to the

everlasting world of the hereafter. To get them to recognise their creator, who created everyone and everything. To carry out our duty towards them. To disclose to them the knowledge that we possess about what happens after death, and what is waiting for all of us there. So that, when they get there, and see for themselves, they have no excuse or complaints against us.

On the other hand, what they invite us to is destruction, immorality, to degrade ourselves, and to be followers of Satan. Their invitation is aimed at taking us out of the light and into the darkness. Where we cannot see what we are doing, or recognise who we are. They know where their way of living, and the road they are following, is leading them to. Destruction, insanity and suicide, and they do not want to go down alone, and leave the Muslims standing up. They aim to take down, with them, as many as they can; this is the plan of their leader, Satan.

The continuous efforts of the disbelievers have paid off, and they have succeeded in taking away many of our Muslim children. They have succeeded to take Muslims wives away from their husbands, husbands away from their wives, parents away from their children. Encouraged, motivated, and provided help to mothers to go away, and leave their children, and for fathers, to go away, and look for fun and enjoyment, away from their families. They made such sources of attractions and enjoyment readily available and easily accessible. They encouraged children and provided them with all the assistance needed to go away and leave their parents, making every effort to prevent them from returning. Whenever the children return, they are never the same children. They have a different identity, implanted into their heart and minds, that can never be removed again. They took Muslim children away, into their Discos, into their nightclubs, to drink alcohol, which is a totally forbidden substance in Islam, into the streets, and into their drug centres. Into their prisons and jails and finally into their graveyards, but never to rest in peace, as they may not have died as Muslims.

Muslim mothers were encouraged to go out to work, as a father working alone was never enough to support the family. They made the wages so low, and the cost of living so high, that no one can live in peace and concentrate on bringing up their family, the way they wanted. Forcing many mothers to go out to work, to help the father support the family, had simply meant, leaving the children for the disbelievers to work on them, again at home, through their media, that invaded the Muslim homes, as if it was not enough for them to work on the Muslim children all day at their schools, they continue to bombard the Muslim children even after they go home, and while the parents are out there trying to earn their living, to support the children. The schools were a non-Islamic environment, which did extensive damage to the Muslim children, and the Muslim home has also become a non-Islamic environment.

While Muslim parents were out there working to get money to feed and clothe their children, the disbelievers were working hard on the Muslim children, with their totally non-Islamic ideology to win them over and alienate them from their parents.

When the parents got home, after working late at night, often the children were not there anymore, or if they were there, they were getting educated, and doctrine, by the most evil device ever created, by the disbelievers, the television, in preparation to get them to leave home.

The parents may have succeeded in getting the double-story house and the flash car, but what sort of children do they have there? And, at what price? One Muslim child lost is the responsibility of the whole Muslim community. Who is going to question you about that? Just wait and see. At that time, you will not be able to argue, like you do now; your tongue will not be the thing that will talk for you, no more arguing, no more lying, no more deceiving, no more excuses, it is time to pay.

Many Muslim families watched silently, while their children were taken away from them, and the disbelievers surrounded the parents with laws, rules and regulations, and sometimes used force to prevent the parents from reaching out for their gone children.

What are the Muslims going to do about their lost children who were taken away from them? What did the Muslim families do to protect their children? Is there any effort made to get our children back and save them from the fire of Hell? More importantly, what efforts are the Muslims making now to protect those who remained with them? How can you protect your children and prevent them from being taken away from you? How can you protect your family? Your home from being invaded? Do you think you still have your children with you? But are they really your children? You may think so, or you would like to think so, but just have a close look and see what you got there. Even if you were one of those blessed ones who have children with Islamic appearance, and your girls wear Hijab, look at what is inside their heads. Especially, if they had attended a public school in this country, which must have corrupted their Islamic way of thinking. As a Muslim, are you content to stand there and watch? Do you not think the time has come for you to protect your children? Your family, your religion? Are you content with what you got? Is your main concern to look after and protect what you have got? If you think that what you got is going to benefit you, after you have gone, then continue to take care of that, and forget about your children, about your family, and about your religion. Do not say that you are doing that for them. How many children do you know of who continued to visit their parents' grave after they died, leaving behind for them a two-story house, a business and the rest? Are you saying you are doing that for them? Is this going to protect them? After you have gone, more invasions of your Muslim home will take place, until it is no longer a Muslim home.

Is this the kind of thing which we as Muslims are required to leave for our children?

If your children encourage you to work hard, so you can secure a good financial future for them, then have a good look to see if they are really your children or your enemy.

If you really brought them up the right way, they would never want to see you going to the fire of Hell because of them, would they?

When your daughter disobeys you and refuses to cover herself, she must know that, by doing this, she is sending you to the fire of Hell? You're saying you are doing that for them, you poor man, what have you done for yourself? What preparation have you made for yourself? What have you got to take with you when you leave? You think you are not going to leave, you are going to stay here forever? Even an atheist does not deny that one day he will have to leave. You think you are a hero? You can stand the punishment, or do you have a proof and a case to present to your creator, that what you were doing was right? You must be sure that, if it is not according to what he ordered and instructed you to do, then it will not be accepted from you. Do not make your own rules and regulations to suit yourself, and then think that you are onto something. Making your own rules and regulations, in itself, is enough to admit you to where those who think like that belong. Wake up now and do something for yourself.

Muslims should wake up and ask themselves, what have the disbelievers done to us? They have succeeded in entering our Muslim homes, breaking our Muslim families, and invading our Muslim faith. Our homes no longer resemble a Muslim home. Our families are no longer an example of Muslim families. Our children do not look like, or cannot be recognised as, Muslim children. Our habits are the habits of the disbelievers, the habits of the people of Hell. Islam is no longer in our homes; it is no longer in our habits. If we speak, we lie; if we promise, we deny, and if we trust, we betray. A brother is killing his own, a mother deserting home, Islam, we do not have you anymore, in any of our homes, Islam, when are you coming back? The whole world is waiting. When are you coming back? Coming back.

Our creator told us, he made an appointment for every one of us, to talk to him and ask all our needs of him, five times a day. We said, " No thanks. I want to ask my Kaffer boss for my needs. I want to ask my machine, my computer, my bucket and mop, which I used to do the job that pays me. I want to ask my Taxi, my Bakery, my Bus, my shop, but not you, my creator. I cannot keep my appointment with you, my creator, five times a day. I am too busy for that. I have to be at the command of those, and those things, which provide for me and bring me sustenance. Praying five times a day, and leaving what I am doing, would result in losing my job, my business and I cannot survive.
The creator has provided for all mankind since he created the earth. He has taken upon himself to provide for all his creations, believers or disbelievers, humans or otherwise. He is providing for all other creations that do not have a job, or a bank account, or receive payment from social security. They are different. Why are they different? Don't they need to eat and drink as well? Have you ever seen an animal starving to death? Or a bird, or an ant? NO, never, but we have seen other human beings dying from starvation, not because the creator did not provide for them, or forgot about them, or did not have enough for them. The creator did provide for them, but other greedy human beings wanted to take their share, or prevent food from getting to them, to get them to bow down and accept certain conditions, or more precisely, to get them to follow another religion.

Under the name of freedom, they made prostitution and drugs spread everywhere, even in Islamic countries. They brought immorality to the whole world through their corrupted and obscene media.
Under the name of freedom, the voices of the disbelievers were heard in the countries of Islam, and they dared to invite Muslims to abandon their religion. Under the name of freedom, they succeeded in entering the countries of Islam and occupied the countries of Islam.

Muslims should reject this kind of evil ideology and return to the real thoughts of their beautiful, peaceful, and clean religion. This is the only way for Muslims to stand back on their feet, by rejecting these kinds of ignorant and illogical ideas, which can only bring destruction and shame to Muslims. God has promised that if Muslims strive in his path, they are guaranteed victory and triumph, and that the troops who carry out the message of God are set to succeed and win. Who can stand against the troops and the soldiers of God?
We as Muslims, when we propagate Islam, we invite people to recognise their creator and understand the real purpose of their existence, to be saved from eternal and severe punishment. We do so because we have been ordered by the creator to invite all mankind towards Islam. We have been instructed to carry out the propagation of this religion, and it is not our concern whether people listen, obey, follow or not. It has been made very clear to us that the guidance of any human being is only in the hands of Allah (swt) alone. Therefore, we do not need to hold the Koran in one hand, and hold food, drink and

money in the other hand, stretching it out, to those dying from hunger and starvation, compelling them to accept the Koran before we can give them the food, the drink and the money, which will save their lives. This is what the disbelievers tried to do in some poor Muslim countries. They held the Bible with one hand, food, drink, and money with the other hand. Their miserable attempts were nothing but doom and failure.
The West sends its Christian missionaries to poor Muslim countries, which have become poor because of the plotting and planning of the offending West. The West planned and plotted to prevent food and drinks from getting to those countries, making them poor, by taking all their mineral resources. When those missionaries go there into these poor Muslim countries, they try unsuccessfully to bribe people, offering them money, to get them to become Christians.

Islam has gone through a stage of the killing of faith inside the hearts of Muslims. This was done by some who considered themselves to be Muslims. They took charge of the Friday congregation. Deviated from talking about the real Islam, instead, they talked about a topic totally unrelated to the faith. Contrary to the requirement of the speech of Friday, which had been designed to lift and strengthen the beliefs of the Muslims, who for the rest of the week engaged in worldly activities. The Friday congregation should provide the Muslims with essential teachings of Islam. The talk should be mainly about death, and a reminder that we are not here forever, and soon will have to leave, and should prepare ourselves for such

a time, and be always ready to meet our creator, and look forward to it.
Hardly any of those who took charge of this are carrying out their responsibilities, according to the instructions of the faith. They have fully occupied themselves with the materialistic means of this world, thus misguiding themselves and those who listen to them.
The true and correct belief was put to sleep inside the hearts of the Muslims by those so-called Muslim Imams, who sold their religion and received their instructions from the West, on how to conduct the Friday speech. If the Friday congregation is carried out correctly and regularly, it would be more than enough to inspire the Muslims and make them stand up against all the odds.
Assigning one Imam for each Mosque, the disbelievers discovered that it is such a dangerous idea. Various Imams for each Mosque will ensure that no single Imam has any control over the masses who attend the prayer in that Mosque. It will ensure that no real bond between an Imam and those who attend that Mosque would exist. It will ensure that a replacement Imam is always there if an Imam goes out of line when giving his speech.

In these difficult times, the disbelievers are united against the Muslims, hoping to put out the light of the guidance of Islam. But the light of Islam will shine over the globe in completion, despite the arrogance and the stubbornness of the disbelievers. They have tried in every way to spread despair in the hearts of Muslims, get the Muslims to concentrate and spend their time looking for their sustenance. The disbelievers told the Muslims, rest, you have been struggling for a very long time. This struggle will not benefit you. You have had enough suffering; do not ask for more. It is time you enjoy this life. Forget your case. Give it up. Do not try to correct. Do not try to moralise. Do not try for justice. You're fighting a losing battle. Why you? All the other Muslims are asleep. The slaughtering of Muslims is happening every day. The norm is to be immoral, to be corrupted. Why are you wasting your time trying to fix things up? Your case is a hopeless one. Join the crowds. You will be better off being with the majority. You're either with us or against us. We will take care of all your needs and remove all your debts. We have the cure for all your problems. Come to us, come to the West.

One of the most serious misconceptions that a Muslim can fall into is to believe that the West is the one that decides in this world. The West has nothing whatsoever to do with deciding what goes on in this world. This world has a creator, and he is the one who decides everything that happens in this world.

We should never try to judge matters with our own intellect or our own way of thinking. The creator has different ways of dealing with different situations that may not be understood by us. But yet it is all his decisions alone.

The disbelievers spend their wealth to prevent Islam from being established on earth. They will succeed in spending their wealth, but at the end, it would be nothing but a disgrace for them, they will be defeated, and to the fire of hell they will be admitted.

The real threats to the Muslim families are the dangers of forgetting the real and true instructions of their faith. Neglecting their duties towards God, and mixing it with other customers, who are foreigners to their beliefs. The result of that will be damaging to their relationship with their creator. That will attract the creator's displeasure. Allah (swt) has promised that in such times, when the Muslims start to follow the footsteps of the disbelievers, then his punishment will fall upon the Muslims, in the form of being disgraced, and having no significant value in the eyes of the disbelievers. Muslims need to take the instructions of their creator very seriously, because this is where their real salvation and their real success lie.

We must have total belief that all of us, one day, will stand in front of Allah (swt), and we must prepare ourselves for that day. On that day, there will be no one to help us, no one to assist us. Everyone has to speak for themselves. The father will not help his son. The mother will not help her daughter. Each one will be worried about themselves. Our purpose, and our objective, in this short life that we have, is to recognise Allah (swt). How can we fulfil the commands of Allah (swt)?
How can every one of us understand the purpose for which Allah (swt) has sent us to this world? Allah (swt) has not sent us to this world to make ourselves comfortable, to build high-rise buildings, to establish big business, to acquire and collect wealth, or to strive for power and fame. For that, Allah (swt) had sent us many prophets to make us understand that our existence in this world is for a purpose and an objective, and we are not here in this world just to pass our time. But our object of coming to this world is to prepare for the hereafter. To prepare to meet

Allah (swt). Allah (swt), before he sent us to this world, has determined the period of our lives, for every one of us in this world. Allah (swt) has determined how much sustenance we are going to get. No person will ever leave this world until they have taken the amount of sustenance that has been allocated for them by Allah (swt).

For that, our purpose in this life is not to acquire our sustenance. Allah (swt) has taken care of our sustenance, of all our needs. But our purpose and object is to recognise Allah (swt). Who is Allah (swt)? Who is this great creator who has created everything? Those that we can see, and those that we cannot see. That Allah (swt), who has created the seven heavens and the seven earths. That Allah (swt), who has created the mountains, the skies, and the oceans. That Allah (swt), who has created me, and you, and everyone else, on this earth, in the best of all forms, and made us, the best of all his creations. Who is this Allah? How much do we know of this Allah (swt)? How much knowledge do you have about Allah? What is the power of Allah (swt)? What is Allah (swt) capable of doing?

Today, we recite this KALIMAH, we say we believe in Allah (swt), but how much conviction do we have in this belief? We, daily in our prayers, say (Ehdena al surat al mustaqueem), guide us to the right path. What is this guidance that we ask Allah (swt) for? It is the guidance we need to recognise Allah (swt). Because we are saying in front of Allah (swt), Oh Allah, it is only you that we worship, and only you that we ask for help. But when the need arises, who do we turn to? Where is our (yaqueen) conviction? Is it on Allah (swt), or on the means? Today, Muslim brothers and sisters, our (yaqueen) is not in Allah (swt). If we have any difficulty or any problems, we immediately turn towards the means. When all the means fail, then we turn to Allah (swt). The Prophet (aesws) has made such an effort, on his companions, to correct their conviction in Allah (swt), to take out from the depths of their hearts, the incorrect belief. The belief that is in our hearts today, that the materials, the things of this world, the conditions around us, these are the things that bring us benefits. We teach our children and train them in such a way that they can acquire degrees and professions, so they can become successful. We teach our children, the incorrect (yaqueen) belief from a small age, that the degrees, the professions and the big business, are what will fulfil our needs. This is the incorrect belief that we must get out of our hearts.

The correct belief is that only Allah (swt) is the doer of everything. We must have the total and full belief that Allah (swt) did not put the success in any of the things that we have in our position. All the things that we have are just creations of Allah (swt). They cannot benefit us, nor can they harm us. Only Allah (swt) can benefit us and harm us. Not the creations of Allah (swt). Things that we see that have benefit in it, Allah (swt), can put harm in it. Things that we see harm in, Allah (swt) can put benefit in it. It is not the actual object that benefits and harms, but what Allah (swt) makes it to be. Two people have the same sickness, and go to the same doctor, who gives them the same medicine, but you find that one is cured, and one dies. It is not the medicine, it is not the doctor, who can benefit, or harm; it is all in the hands of Allah (swt). Allah (swt) will give benefit to whoever he wants to give benefit to, and will give harm to whoever he wants to give harm to. This is the effort that we have to make in our hearts, to correct our Yaqueen in Allah (swt). Allah (swt) will forgive every sin, except (SHIRK), attaching partners with Allah (swt). If we check in our lives, every one of us, in some form or another, is making SHIRK.

We say, I am doing this, I am doing that, this is my business, this is my house, this is my wealth, when nothing belongs to us.

Everything belongs to Allah (swt), and Allah (swt) can give to whom he wants and take from whoever he wants. We have to talk about this, again and again, until this firm belief that Allah (swt) is the doer of everything comes to our hearts. Every day of our lives, we have to speak so much about Allah and his greatness and power. All the problems that we face today are because this firm believes that Allah has not entered our hearts. We can see what the companions of the Prophet were capable of doing when this firm belief and trust in Allah (swt) entered their hearts. They never turned to the means, but to the power of Allah (swt). In the Battle of Bader, when the companions were fewer in number. 313, could hardly stand up, because of hunger and thirst, had no weapons to fight with, against a huge, strong, fully equipped army of 1000 of the disbelievers.

The companions never looked at their own condition or the enemy's condition but looked at the power of Allah (swt), and Allah (swt), gave them victory and success. But, we find in the battle of Honain, when for the first time, the Muslims were more in number, some of the young companions, who had just embraced Islam, came to their minds that today we are greater in number, so we should overpower the disbelievers, without any trouble. When that thought came to their hearts, Allah's help was immediately withdrawn from them.

For that, we should have total Yaqueen in Allah (swt), and we should not look at the conditions around us. The conditions around us could be against us, could be most unfavourable, so long as our trust is in Allah (swt), then Allah's help is with us. It is Allah's promise. If our beliefs and our convictions are in our business, or jobs, or our professions, then Allah (swt) will leave us to our businesses, to our jobs, and to our professions. If our belief and conviction are in Allah (swt), then Allah (swt) will provide for us and take care of our needs. Allah (swt) will treat us according to our expectations of him. Allah (swt) provided for Ibrahim when he was in the fire for forty days. provided for Juno, when he was inside the tomb of the whales, for forty days. Provided for the people of the cave for three hundred and nine years, and sustained them while they were asleep and without even having to open their mouths. Allah (swt) has provided for Bani Israel, for forty years, their children were born with cloths on them, and when the children grew, their cloths grew on them; they did not have to make any effort to sustain themselves. The same Allah who provides for them can provide for us. The only difference is our convection, which is not in Allah (swt). It is not our efforts and what we are doing in our jobs that are sustaining us. It is Allah (swt) who is sustaining us. When Allah (swt) spoke to Mussa and told him to go to the Pharaoh, and invite him to believe in Allah, Mussa (AES), asked Allah who was going to look after his wife, who was sick and expecting a child? Allah (swt). Allah (swt) wanted to teach us a lesson, asked Mussa to hit a big rock, then Mussa hit the rock, and the rock split in half, and inside the rock was another smaller rock, Allah (swt) asked Mussa to hit this rock, and Mussa did, and inside that rock was another rock, Allah (swt) asked Mussa to also hit this rock, and Mussa did, and inside that third rock a little insect was eating tiny green leaf. Inside the rock, that hard rock, Allah (swt) has sustained that little insect that was praising Allah (swt), and saying Allah (swt) did not forget me. This is the yaqueen that we should have, that Allah (swt) is providing for all his creations. The insects, the animals and the birds have no jobs, but Allah (swt) is providing for them. Allah (swt) provides for all the creations that have their trust in him, whether they are at the bottom of the oceans or in the middle of the skies. This is the biggest problem that is facing us today: how are we going to get our sustenance, and who will provide for us? When we stand in front of Allah (swt), our first worry and concern is our needs, our (Rezek) sustenance. This is the thing that is holding us back from committing ourselves to Allah (swt). The majority of the companions of the Prophet were very poor; they did not know where the next meal was coming from, but that did not prevent them from having full trust and full belief in Allah (swt). The companions did not learn this belief at any school, any university or any Dar El-Eloom. They acquire this Yaqueen by only striving in his path to establish his Dean (religion) on earth. Allah (swt) in all the stories of the Prophets, mentioned in the Koran, did not talk about how much worship these prophets made for Allah (swt). Allah (swt) talks about all the efforts they made in calling people towards Allah (swt). This is the only means that will bring us closer to Allah (swt). All the things around us are deceiving us; we have to correct our belief in Allah (swt) before we leave this world, before we enter our grave, and get asked who is your Lord? Who was sustaining you? Who did you turn to in this world? At that time, it will be sealed, and whatever in our hearts will come out. So if we do not make efforts to correct what is in our hearts, then may Allah save us.

The cure and remedies for all the problems, physical, mental, emotional, or financial is for the soul to be connected with its owner, with its creator. You may continue to suffer from illness, but you have enough patience to endure the pain. You may not become a millionaire overnight, but with the few dollars you may have in your pocket, you would be content. To overcome all sadness, grief, and anxiety, the soul needs to be connected with its source, where it originated, or it will continue to suffer until it returns to its source.

What the greats need that Muslims need today is HEDAIA (guidance), more than food and drink. In order to get this guidance, an effort is required so that this religion can come alive in the whole world. For this religion to become alive, in the whole world, the wives of the companions were made widows, the children of the companions were made orphans, and through their efforts, we are Muslims today.

Today, the commands of Allah (swt) are broken before our own eyes, and we are quite happy with that. The companions were very content with what little they had; all their attentions were directed towards the hereafter, sending all their actions to be deposited there for them. We are very discontent with all that we have, and we want to have more; all our attention is directed towards this world. How much are we doing for the hereafter?

If you love someone, would you be eager and looking forward to meeting that someone, whom you love? How many of us Muslims are looking forward to meeting Allah (swt)?

True contentment lies in the heart and in understanding life: why you are here and what you should be doing. This understanding brings great comfort—knowing that Allah exists, that there is a God whom you worship and obey. In human terms, it means knowing that, in His sight, you are doing what is right. You no longer need to rely on your own moral compass; you have been given clear guidance that defines what is right and what is wrong. Acting upon this knowledge brings inner peace and leads to better relationships with others.

Inner Faith and Unassailable Conviction

Islam teaches that true strength lies not in worldly power but in faith rooted in the heart.

“Verily, in the remembrance of Allah do hearts find rest.”

(Qur’an 13:28)

A believer carries faith wherever he goes. No external force can strip it away.

“And whoever relies upon Allah—then He is sufficient for him.”

(Qur’an 65:3)

Islam recognises that moral decay is often more destructive than physical force:

“And do not follow the footsteps of Shayṭān. Indeed, he is to you a clear enemy.”

(Qur’an 2:168)

The Prophet ﷺ warned:
“The world is sweet and green, and Allah has put you in charge of it to see how you will act.” (Sahih Muslim)

When Muslims internalise false portrayals and lose confidence, division follows:
“And do not dispute and [thus] lose courage and your strength departs.”

(Qur’an 8:46)

The Prophet ﷺ said:
“The nations will gather against you as people gather to eat from a bowl.”

They asked: *“Because we will be few?”*

He replied: *"No, you will be many, but you will be like foam on the sea."*
(Sunan Abu Dawood)

Muslim Accountability and Moral Reversal
The Qur'an repeatedly reminds Muslims to correct themselves first:
"Indeed, Allah will not change the condition of a people until they change what is in themselves."
(Qur'an 13:11)

One of the gravest warnings is moral inversion:
"You enjoin what is right and forbid what is wrong…"
(Qur'an 3:110)

The Prophet ﷺ warned:
"When people see wrongdoing and do not stop it, Allah may punish them all."
(Sunan al-Tirmidhi)

Muslim Accountability and Moral Reversal
The Qur'an repeatedly reminds Muslims to correct themselves first:
"Indeed, Allah will not change the condition of a people until they change what is in themselves."
(Qur'an 13:11)

One of the gravest warnings is moral inversion:
"You enjoin what is right and forbid what is wrong…"
(Qur'an 3:110)

The Prophet ﷺ warned:
"When people see wrongdoing and do not stop it, Allah may punish them all."
(Sunan al-Tirmidhi)

(15)

TO THE DISBELIEVERSE
Even if You Burn The Qur'an, We will Not Burn The Bible

To the disbelievers
"What can my enemies do to me?
My paradise is in my heart.
If they imprison me, my prison is seclusion with my Lord.
If they exile me, my exile is a journey with my Lord.
If they kill me, my death is martyrdom."
"What can my enemies do to me?

What did the **kuffār** (disbelievers) do to eliminate Islam?
They planned to pull Muslims away from Islam—to eliminate any connection between the teachings of Islam and the Muslims themselves. They sought to

remove all ties between Muslims and their faith, to corrupt them morally and ethically, to make them dishonest, deceptive, and without manners, and to destroy any sense of belonging between Muslims and their religion.

They aimed to make Muslims so insignificant that they would have no value in their own eyes or in the eyes of others. Through their corrupted media—eager and waiting—they presented Muslims in distorted images, painting them with the colours of blood, ignorance, and alienation from the rest of the world. They made sure that Muslims themselves saw these images before non-Muslims did, so that Muslims would lose confidence in themselves and in their faith, creating division and factions among them. Some stood up to the challenge and defended their faith with all the strength they had, while others accepted and submitted to the opinions of the disbelievers, blaming Islam and Muslims for conditions that were, in reality, manufactured by the media.

The disbelievers planned to push Muslims toward destructive and immoral habits. They placed wine and prostitution before them, believing—correctly—that corruption of the heart is more effective than pointing guns at chests. They sought to drown Muslims in alcohol and adultery to sever their connection with their Creator. To the disbelievers, a Muslim disconnected from his Creator is far more useful for their plans than one of their own.

They planned to separate Islam from politics and to divide religion from governance. They replaced the commands of the Creator with man-made constitutions that paralyse Islamic teachings and laws. They introduced the Western democratic system to challenge Islam and used all their power to export it worldwide, aiming to prevent Muslims from being governed by Islam. They realised that Islam could not be removed except by destroying the bond between Muslims and their Creator.

Muslims gradually accepted wrongdoing around them and accepted that correcting it was not their responsibility. Worse still, many began to participate in wrongdoing, encourage it, and reverse moral values—calling wrong right and right wrong. Some even began commanding evil and forbidding good, defeating the very purpose for which Muslims were created: to bring guidance for themselves and for all mankind.

The results are clear today in the condition, status, and position of Muslims worldwide. The disbelievers succeeded in distancing Muslims from their religion, and as a consequence, God abandoned them—as He promised—handing them over to punishment if they failed to fulfil their role.

Muslims who once knew who God is, what Islam is, and who their Prophet is abandoned all of that to follow the path of the disbelievers. In the sight of God, such people are worse than disbelievers themselves. Some Muslims were impressed by the power and manipulation of disbelievers, forgetting the power of their Almighty Creator. The Prophet of Islam passed away over 1,400 years ago, yet his message is more alive today than ever. There is not a single place on earth where the call to prayer is not proclaimed five times daily. During the Prophet's lifetime, this call was limited to his homeland; today it echoes across lands he never knew, spoken by people of every race and colour.

Since the Prophet's death, Islam has continued to grow and will do so until the Last Day. No one can stop it, for God has promised that this religion will prevail over all others.

The task of ensuring Islam's prevalence was never dependent on Muslims themselves; this is why the condition of Muslims does not hinder the spread of Islam. Muslims who choose to follow disbelievers only harm themselves—Islam remains untouched. God has promised to replace those Muslims with others who love Him, establish prayer, worship sincerely, and strive to uphold His commands on earth.

The efforts of disbelievers have always been in vain. Is it not time for misguided Muslims to realise this—to return to their Creator with repentance, tears, regret, and fear of God rather than fear of people? What belief will they meet Him with? God has clearly stated that any belief other than Islam will not be accepted in the Hereafter.

Islam has never been a religion that could be defeated. When early disbelievers failed to stop the Prophet, they proposed compromise: worship each other's religion alternately. The response was the revelation of **Surah Al-Kāfirūn**:

"O disbelievers, I do not worship what you worship…
You have your religion, and I have mine."

Today, when all else has failed, the same proposal reappears under new names. The call to prayer never stops—it only moves across the earth with the turning of day and night. "God is Great" is proclaimed every second somewhere on this planet.

Despite their advanced technology, disbelievers know Islam is not man-made, yet arrogance prevents submission. They attempt to borrow Islamic principles while denying their source, promoting the idea that "all religions are the same."

Islam belongs to no race or nationality. It is for all mankind. All prophets called to Islam. Whoever sincerely investigates will be guided.

Islam will not be harmed whether all people accept it or reject it. The decision is individual—but irreversible after death. No one returns to correct their belief.

Everything in the universe serves mankind; mankind was created to serve God by submitting to Him. His blessings are countless. Who would exchange eyesight for all the wealth of the world?

Man proudly boasts of technology, yet cannot stop storms, earthquakes, floods, or volcanoes. He stands powerless before God's creation—just as he will stand on the Day of Judgment.

Technology increases fear without providing control. Knowledge shifts from man to machines, leaving humanity more vulnerable than before.

Every human admits he did not create himself. Yet he defies the One who did. Such arrogance blinds him to truth.

All humans believe in death—an unseen reality. Why then reject other unseen truths? The search for God cannot be delayed.

Whoever sincerely seeks guidance will be guided. Those who refuse will awaken only after death—when it is too late.

Islam is our life. Everything we do is according to Islam—eating, drinking, sleeping, marriage, birth, and death. Even disbelievers have rights upon us under Islam.
Why do the disbelievers scheme to prevent Muslims from practicing this beautiful religion? Yet the door of mercy remains open to every soul, but Allah's guidance reaches whom He wills.

The Qur'an sets a challenge to the whole of mankind. If you don't believe that this book is the word of God, then just produce one verse like it in the same style and the same transparency, and seek the help of all your supporters if you are truthful.
Of all these people who say the Qur'an is not real, Allah does not exist, Muhammad made it all up, they have lengthy debates for hours and hours, but they won't do this one simple challenge, how long can it take them, but in 1440 years, not one person has been able to do this.
Allah goes on to say you will not be able to write a verse like it, and to anyone out there that doubting Islam, take this challenge: come forth and bring a verse.

Attempts to Distance Muslims from Islam
The Qur'an openly acknowledges that there will always be attempts to divert believers from their faith: **"They wish that you would disbelieve as they disbelieved so you would be alike."** (Qur'an 4:89)

Such efforts historically include moral corruption, ideological confusion, and social pressure:

"They will continue to fight you until they turn you back from your religion, if they are able." (Qur'an 2:217)

Media, Misrepresentation, and Internal Weakening

Islam teaches that false images and narratives influence hearts:

"They distort words from their proper places." (Qur'an 5:13)

Separation of Religion from Life and Governance

Islam rejects the separation of faith from life:

"Say: Indeed, my prayer, my sacrifice, my living and my dying are for Allah, Lord of the worlds." (Qur'an 6:162)

Replacing divine guidance with purely human legislation is warned against:

"And whoever does not judge by what Allah has revealed—then it is those who are the wrongdoers."
(Qur'an 5:45)

Islam does not deny governance or systems, but insists that justice must be rooted in divine guidance.

Islam's Continuity and Divine Protection

Islam's survival is not dependent on people:

"Indeed, We have sent down the Reminder, and indeed, We will guard it."
(Qur'an 15:9)

The Prophet ﷺ said:
"This matter will reach wherever the night and day reach."
(Musnad Ahmad)

The call to prayer continuing worldwide reflects this promise.

No Compromise in Belief
The Qur'an decisively rejects theological compromise:
"Say: O disbelievers,

I do not worship what you worship…
For you is your religion, and for me is mine."
(Qur'an 109:1–6)

Peaceful coexistence does not require dilution of faith.

Universality of Islam
Islam is not ethnic or national:
"We have not sent you except as a mercy to all the worlds."
(Qur'an 21:107)

All prophets called to submission to One God:
"Indeed, the religion in the sight of Allah is Islam."
(Qur'an 3:19)

The Prophet ﷺ said:
"All prophets are brothers; their religion is one."
(Sahih al-Bukhari)

Technology and Human Limitation
Islam acknowledges human advancement while reminding of its limits:
"You have been given of knowledge only a little."
(Qur'an 17:85)

Natural forces remain beyond human control:
"And none knows the soldiers of your Lord except Him."
(Qur'an 74:31)

Creation, Arrogance, and Accountability
Man did not create himself:
"Was man created from nothing, or was he the creator [of himself]?"
(Qur'an 52:35)

Arrogance is condemned:
"Indeed, He does not like the arrogant."
(Qur'an 16:23)

Belief in the Unseen
Faith begins with belief in the unseen:
"This is the Book... a guidance for those who believe in the unseen."
(Qur'an 2:2–3)

Death is certain:
"Every soul shall taste death."
(Qur'an 3:185)

And accountability follows:
"Then you will surely be asked that Day about pleasure."
(Qur'an 102:8)

Seeking Guidance
Guidance is promised to sincere seekers:
"And those who strive for Us—We will surely guide them to Our ways."
(Qur'an 29:69)

Delay is dangerous:
"Until, when death comes to one of them, he says: 'My Lord, return me…' No."
(Qur'an 23:99–100)

Final Invitation
This message is not coercion:
"There is no compulsion in religion."
(Qur'an 2:256)

It is an invitation to reflection, truth, and salvation.
"Whoever seeks a religion other than Islam, it will never be accepted from him."
(Qur'an 3:85)

Islam invites you—not to follow people—but to know your Creator.

Read. Reflect. Ask. Seek.
Guidance is for those who want it.
An example of how Allah (swt) describes the attitude of the disbeliever is stated in this verse from the Quran:

"there are some among them who lend you their ears,
but they are dull of hearing and their hearts are muffled,
so nothing penetrates into their mind.
Let them be shown any sign, they will not believe.
They come to you only to dispute.
And the disbelievers among them
dismiss what you tell them as nothing but old tales.
They do not allow themselves to be persuaded by truth
and dissuade the others too.
But do not think that they harm your case,
they only harm themselves, though they do not know.
Imagine them standing on the brink of Hell
when they will say: if only we could
return to earth, we will join the believers,
and defy the signs of God no more. Not that they mean this.
What else can they say confronted with what they denied?
Were they to be sent back, they
will do exactly what they used to do. They are but liars.
Here they claim; this is the only life we have
and we shall not be raised after we die.
If only you could see them arraigned before their Lord,
"Is this not the truth?" He will ask,
and they will submit, 'Yes, O Lord.'
'Well then', He will ordain, 'suffer
now the consequences of your disbelieve.'

Lost are those who deny the return to
God till the hour is upon them.
Then they exclaim; oh, what a terrible mistake we made!
There they are with their sins on their backs.
Look, what a frightful burden they bear!
Life is but transient pleasure.
The Hereafter is a better abode for the righteous.
Do you not understand this?
We know you are grieved by what they say.
They denounce not you but the message of God.
Before you too the prophets were denounced.
But they suffered patiently till We came to their rescue.
No one can change the words of God.
And you know something of what the prophets had to go through.
Do you find the indifference of the people unbearable?
Then, if you have the strength, raise a ladder to the sky
or dig a tunnel into the earth and
find them some convincing proof?
Had God willed it so they would, all have submitted to guidance.
SURA AL- ANAM (25 to 35)

(16)

WHY ISLAM?
The System of Justice

This Book, “the Qur’an”, contains all the guidance needed for all mankind

Islam is a religion ordained by the Creator of all mankind, and Muhammad ﷺ is the final messenger to humanity. After him, there will be no other prophet. Allah revealed this truth more than 1,400 years ago, and ever since, disbelievers have tried to prove Allah wrong. Have they succeeded? No. No one has ever been able to challenge what Allah has declared, and no one ever will, because Allah is the Truth.

Having failed to challenge Allah after all these centuries, the West’s remaining option is submission to Him. Across the world, people have had more than enough of the Western system of government. They are tired of being lied to, deceived, mistreated, misled, oppressed, and victimised.

Under this system, people’s right to live a decent life has been violated. They are encouraged to live indecent, immoral, and shameful lives. As a result, people are searching for a way out—for a real alternative. They are waiting for real change, one that will bring an end to the chaos the world is experiencing today.

That alternative is Islam. It is a complete system of justice, fairness, decency, morality, honesty, and integrity. It contains no discrimination, no bias, and no prejudice. It is the system of Allah.

Islam is the only system fit to legislate for all of mankind—politically, socially, economically, and most importantly, spiritually. It is the only system capable of confronting oppressive, violent, and incompetent systems of governance that have produced nothing but corruption and injustice across the world.

The Western way of life has brought shame, indecency, immorality, and destruction upon humanity.

Inevitably, Islam will return to govern the world, and it is already on its way. No one can stop it—not with power, not with technology, and not even if they were to spend all their wealth and mobilise all their forces. This is the will of Allah.

Allah is our Creator. He has explained to us, step by step, how He created us—how our bodies are formed from the moment a woman conceives until a child is born. No one else has claimed responsibility for the creation of mankind and the universe except Allah.

Allah has declared that He alone gives life and He alone takes it away by His decree. Therefore, He alone has the authority to tell us how to live and to legislate laws and rules. Human beings are incapable of legislating justly. They are weak, driven by desire, and unable to do justice even to themselves—so how could they do justice for others?

The Western system is built upon a single ideology: the accumulation of wealth. In pursuit of this goal, they lie, cheat, deceive their own people, and strip them of what is rightfully theirs.

Under this system, people suffer deprivation and are denied their share of their country's wealth.

Under the Islamic system, a leader seeks ways to give to the people, to serve them, to meet their needs, and to protect their interests. He does not eat while one of his subjects remains hungry. In contrast, under Western systems, leaders often seek ways to take from their own people, denying them their rights and entitlements.

ʿUmar ibn al-Khaṭṭāb, a renowned ruler in Islamic history, once encountered a man begging in the street. He asked him which of the People of the Book he belonged to. The man replied that he was a Jew. When ʿUmar asked why he was begging, the man said it was due to old age and need. ʿUmar immediately took him to the public treasury and ordered an allowance for him and for all others in similar circumstances.

On another occasion, ʿUmar heard a baby crying and asked the mother why. She explained that she was trying to wean the child early because allowances were only given once children began eating solid food. ʿUmar immediately changed the policy so that allowances would be granted from the moment a child was born.

Muslim governors sought ways to distribute wealth, not to enrich themselves while their people lived in poverty.

The system of Islam delivers justice not only to Muslims but also—most notably—to non-Muslims. Allah is free from desire, weakness, and prejudice. His attribute is absolute justice for all His creation in this world, while matters of belief are ultimately judged in the Hereafter.

What is authentically established about non-Muslim rights?
Authentic principles from Qur'an and Sunnah

1. **Protection of life and property**

"Whoever kills a muʿāhid (a non-Muslim under covenant) shall not smell the fragrance of Paradise."
— Ṣaḥīḥ al-Bukhārī

2. **Justice and fairness**

"Do not let the hatred of a people prevent you from being just."
— Qur'an 5:8

3. **Kindness and good conduct**

"Allah does not forbid you from being kind and just to those who do not fight you because of religion."
— Qur'an 60:8

4. **Fulfillment of covenants**

"Whoever harms a dhimmī, I will be his opponent on the Day of Resurrection."
— Reported by al-Ṭabarānī (ḥasan according to many scholars)

5. **Freedom of religion**

"There is no compulsion in religion."
— Qur'an 2:256

6. **Legal equality in courts**

7. **Social dignity and safety**

Non-Muslims under Muslim rule were entitled to security, livelihood, and honour.

As Muslims, we are mindful of Allah and of the Day of Judgment. We believe we will be held accountable for every action. We are conscious of the rights Allah has ordained for non-Muslims—even after their death, their bodies must be respected and never mutilated. We do not desecrate the dead bodies of our enemies. We do not burn their books. If others burn the Qur'an, we do not burn the Bible.

We are Muslims. Our mission is to guide humanity to the truth by conveying the message of Islam, regardless of who people are or how they live.

All human beings were created by Allah. No one else created them. Therefore, we must never judge a person by their appearance, clothing, lifestyle, or habits. Who are you to judge who is worthy of guidance? Is it you who guides, or Allah? Leave guidance to Him; your duty is to invite.

Non-Muslims have rights over Muslims, and those rights were ordained by Allah Himself. Among the greatest of these rights is the right to be invited to Islam.

Allah wants to give disbelievers every opportunity to reach the truth so that they are not left in eternal loss. Sometimes, simple actions are enough—declining alcohol, fasting, praying. These differences may spark questions in the hearts of others, by the will of Allah.

Allah commanded Muslims to invite non-Muslims to Islam and promised immense reward for this effort.

The Qur'an is the Book of Allah. It speaks the truth and exposes attempts to conceal it. Yet Allah has promised that His Light will be completed and that Islam will prevail over all other beliefs.

After failing through violence, the West has shifted to non-violent tactics in its opposition to Islam. What it has failed to understand is that Islam cannot be defeated—not because of tactics, but because it is divinely protected.

No matter the methodology, power, technology, wealth, or forces employed, Islam will continue to spread. The sooner this reality is understood, the sooner futile losses will end.

Islam is a religion that cannot be fought or eradicated. Allah has ordained that it will remain until the end of time.

Why All This Fear of Islam?

Attempts are continually made to isolate and single out the Muslim community, and to frighten the wider public away from it. This fear is driven by the concern that more people may come to discover that Islam offers an explanation of ultimate truth—of what this world is, what it means, and where humanity is headed.

Why is Islam feared so intensely? Why is the Muslim community persistently isolated, surveilled, and vilified?

The answer is neither accidental nor benign. Fear is manufactured—carefully and deliberately—to keep the public at a distance from Islam, lest more people discover that it speaks with clarity about truth, justice, purpose, and the ultimate destiny of humanity. A population kept fearful does not ask questions; it obeys narratives.

Islam is a religion that defines rights, including the rights of non-believers, with moral precision. Yet to suppress Islam, Muslims must first be dehumanised.

They are depicted as rigid, backward, uncivilised, and incompatible with Western life. This caricature is repeated endlessly until exclusion appears reasonable and rejection seems necessary.

Muslims are branded *fanatics*, *extremists*, and *radicals*—labels freely used by political leaders in this country as recently as 2025. Strikingly, such language is rarely condemned as hate speech or recognised as provocation, despite its clear role in normalising hostility toward an entire religious community.

One former Australian prime minister publicly declared, *"The problem is Islam."* A current opposition leader from the same political lineage continues to invoke the phrase *"radical Islam"* as if repetition alone can transform falsehood into fact. These figures fade into political obscurity, yet Islam remains—unchanged, unshaken, and enduring.

Islam is not a spectrum of acceptable and unacceptable versions. It is one faith, with one moral foundation. It is not radical, not extremist, and not fanatical. Those who insist otherwise reveal not insight, but ignorance. To attach criminal acts or political agendas to Islam is not analysis—it is incitement. It invites fear, resentment, and ultimately violence against Muslims themselves.

Under the pretext of security, Western governments have expanded legal powers that allow Muslims to be detained, surveilled, and imprisoned without genuine due process. In any system that claims to uphold democratic principles, such laws would be recognised as authoritarian. Instead, they are enforced by justice systems increasingly aligned with executive power.

Midnight raids on Muslim homes have become routine. Homes are entered, families terrorised, and lives destabilised—often without evidence and with no convictions to follow. Authorities frequently anticipate this outcome in advance, yet proceed regardless. Why? Because the objective is not justice, but damage. Reputations are destroyed, communities are intimidated, and fear is reinforced.

To believe that such oppression can continue indefinitely without accountability is a profound delusion. The Creator who witnesses every injustice has promised a day of reckoning. Every tyrant, every enabler, and every silent collaborator will be called to account. There will be no ambiguity then—only justice.

What we are witnessing today—mass displacement, crimes against humanity, and the systematic erasure of entire populations—is not the defence of civilisation. It is the final expression of a moral order built on exploitation, domination, and military supremacy. History shows that systems sustained by injustice do not endure.

Islam has outlived empires before. It will outlive this one too.

(17)

MEET YOUR DEATH
The Journey You Have to Take

Today, we are going to go on a journey—a trip that everyone must join and take part in. There is no choice; it is compulsory, more compulsory than most people realise. You have been told about it, and you have no option but to take it.

What is the name of this trip? Let us call it **the journey of death**.

Imagine yourself acting in a movie called *The Journey of Death*. You are the only actor, and everyone around you is watching as you travel on this journey.

How does this journey start? What happens when you begin to take part in the journey of death and finally meet death?

So, what is death?

Death is something that exists. Death is a creation; it is something that has been created. Death is something you must experience. One day, it will meet you, and you will ask it, *What are you? What are you doing to me?*

And you will be told:

"I am death. I am here for you to experience me. I am here to carry out a physical process on you—to change you from life to another state that defines my name. In seconds, I will leave my mark on you, and you will be called dead."

What if I do not want to take part in this movie?

No—you cannot refuse. Everyone must take part. Now it is your turn. You were told again and again that it is compulsory. In your life, you accepted many compulsory duties and understood what the word *compulsory* meant. Now it is time for this final compulsory act.

Can I have a little time to get ready before my state is changed?

No. This is a timed process—a countdown, a blast-off. It has never been delayed for anyone, and it will never be delayed for anyone.

Can I tell someone about some important matters I was planning to attend to?

If it concerns your bank account, business, studies, marriage or divorce, cancelling another trip, selling your car, or calling your boss to say you are not coming back—do not worry. Those who still have time will deal with these matters. You no longer have time. Any benefit from them will go to others. Nothing can be given to you, sent to you, or transferred to you.

Can I at least say goodbye to my family and friends?

No, that is not allowed.

Just one phone call to my best friend?

It is too late. And let me tell you something—this is a bad sign if you believe you are leaving your best friend behind.

Why is that a bad sign?

Because if you understood your role now, you would realise that your best companion is going with you.

But I do not see anyone going with me.
Do not worry. Everything has been recorded—every small thing and every great thing you have done. The companion you are taking with you is the one you made in this life. This is your true companion.

Your Companion
You may have looked at your companion from time to time. You may have thought it was good, or you may have known it was bad, yet you did nothing to change it. Whether you were aware or unaware, the final result is what you created, and that is what you will take with you. You cannot change it now.
If it is a good companion, you would want to keep it. If it is a bad one, do you really think anyone else would want to take it from you?
Your companion is **your deeds**—your own actions. They belong to you alone. They cannot be inherited or transferred. You should have cared for them instead of focusing on worldly matters that you are now leaving behind.
You now realise that you misunderstood your role in the previous movie called *Life*. You acted with many others, but you neglected to build your companion properly. You filled it with lies, deception, cheating, backbiting, and manipulation—perhaps to serve your own interests or to please others.
Now you must face what you created with your own hands.
Your companion will speak on your behalf before the court you are about to face. If it is corrupt, it will testify against you. You will not be allowed to speak—only your deeds will speak. If your deeds are righteous, they will defend you and call for your reward.

Your companion has recorded everything—even what you forgot.

The Beginning of the Journey

Now your compulsory journey begins.

Those around you will soon realise that you are no longer moving or speaking. They will call you dead. Some may praise you; others may feel relieved that you are gone. Their words will matter.

Nothing will be packed for you. Everything is left behind—your clothes, possessions, certificates, phone, wealth, status.

You leave alone.

You are taken to a new home, where you will remain for a long time, until every human being joins you and no one remains on earth.

This home has no lights, no sounds, no communication, no emergency services.

Waiting for you are two representatives sent by your Creator, who gave you life, provided for you, and has now called you back.

Before you enter, your new home examines your companion.

If your deeds are beautiful, the home becomes beautiful.

If they are ugly and foul, the home prepares punishment.

Your family covers you with earth. The last light disappears. You hear their footsteps fade away. You call out, but they cannot hear you. You are alone—with your deeds.

The Interrogation
The two angels arrive.
If you are a believer, you answer without hesitation:

- **Who is your Lord?** Allah.
- **What is your religion?** Islam.
- **Who is your Prophet?** Muhammad ﷺ.

Your prayers, fasting, charity, and remembrance surround you to protect you.
A window is opened—you see Hell and are told you were saved from it.
Another window opens—you see Paradise and are told this is your place.
But if you fail—if you worshipped wealth, power, desires, or rejected the guidance—you will see Paradise denied and Hell shown as your final destination.
Your grave becomes either a garden of Paradise or a pit of Hell until the Day of Judgment.

Reflection
Today, I am still here. I have looked at my companion, and it does not look beautiful. Do I still have time to fix it?
If I have any wisdom, I must focus on my deeds. I must return rights, correct wrongs, pray, fast, repent, and prepare.
There is no second chance.
Death is the only true reality. Everything else is illusion.
Those who forget death live carelessly. Those who remember it prepare.
The wise person prepares **now**, not later.

www.ingramcontent.com/pod-product-compliance
Lightning Source LLC
Chambersburg PA
CBHW022143050726
47590CB00002B/562

* 9 7 8 0 6 4 6 7 3 5 1 4 6 *